DATE			

CARING FOR ANIMALS
OPPORTUNITIES TO VOLUNTEER

by Bernard Ryan, Jr.

Ryan, Bernard, 1923-
    Community service for teens: opportunities to volunteer / Bernard
Ryan, Jr.
        p. cm.
    Includes bibliographical references and index.
    Contents: [1] Caring for animals -- [2] Expanding education and
literacy -- [3] Helping the ill, the poor & the elderly -- [4] Increasing
neighborhood service -- [5] Participating in government --
- -[6] Promoting the arts and sciences -- [7] Protecting the environment
- -[8] Serving with police, fire & EMS
        ISBN 0-89434-227-4 (v. 1). -- ISBN 0-89434-231-2 (v. 2). -- ISBN
0-89434-229-0 (v. 3). -- ISBN 0-89434-233-9 (v. 4). --
ISBN 0-89434-230-4 (v. 5). -- ISBN 0-89434-234-7 (v. 6). --
ISBN 0-89434-228-2 (v. 7). -- ISBN 0-89434-232-0 (v. 8)
        1. Voluntarism—United States—Juvenile literature. 2. Young
volunteers—United States—Juvenile literature. 3. Teenage
volunteers in social service—United States—Juvenile literature.
[1. Voluntarism.] I. Title.
HN90.V64R93 1998
361.3'7'08350973—dc21

                                                                    97-34971
                                                                         CIP
                                                                          AC

Community Service for Teens: Caring for Animals: Opportunities to Volunteer

A New England Publishing Associates Book
Copyright ©1998 by Ferguson Publishing Company
ISBN 0-89434-227-4

Published and distributed by
Ferguson Publishing Company
200 West Madison, Suite 300
Chicago, Illinois 60606
800-306-9941
Web Site: http://www.fergpubco.com

Printed in the United States of America
V-3

CONTENTS

INTRODUCTION

WHO VOLUNTEERS?

Six out of ten American teenagers work as volunteers. A 1996 survey revealed that the total number of teen volunteers aged 12 to 17 is 13.3 million. They give 2.4 billion hours each year. Of that time, 1.8 billion hours are spent in "formal" commitments to nonprofit organizations. Informal help, like "just helping neighbors," receives 600 million hours.

Each "formal" volunteer gives an average of three and a half hours a week. It would take nearly 1.1 million full-time employees to match these hours. And if the formal volunteers were paid minimum wage for their time, the cost would come to at least $7.7 billion—a tremendous saving to nonprofit organizations.

Only 16 out of 100 volunteers go to schools that insist on community service before graduation.

Teen volunteerism is growing. In the four years between the 1996 survey and a previous one, the number of volunteers grew by 7 percent and their hours increased by 17 percent.

Equal numbers of girls and boys give their time to volunteering.

How voluntary is volunteering? Only 16 out of 100 volunteers go to schools that insist on community service before graduation. Twenty-six out of 100 are in schools that offer courses requiring community service if you want credit for the course.

Six out of ten teen volunteers started volunteering before they were 14 years old. Seventy-eight percent of teens who volunteer have parents who volunteer.

WHY VOLUNTEER?

When teens are asked to volunteer, the 1996 survey revealed, nine out of ten do so. Who does the asking? Usually it's a friend, teacher, family member, relative or church member.

Teens gave a number of reasons for volunteering, regardless of whether their schools required community service. Their reasons included:

(V. Harlow)

Teen volunteering is on the rise throughout the United States. High Hopes Therapeutic Riding, Inc., of Old Lyme, Connecticut, offers various programs to people with all types of disabilities and has more than 200 volunteers in its organization, many of them teenagers. Pauline C. Knoll, volunteer coordinator, stands next to one of the horses, with Terry Balough, adult volunteer, and Kirin Paegler, teen rider.

- You feel compassion for people in need.
- You feel you can do something for a cause that is important to you.
- You believe that if you help others, others will help you.
- Your volunteering is important to people you respect.
- You learn to relate to others who may be different from you.
- You develop leadership skills.
- You become more patient.
- You gain a better understanding of good citizenship.

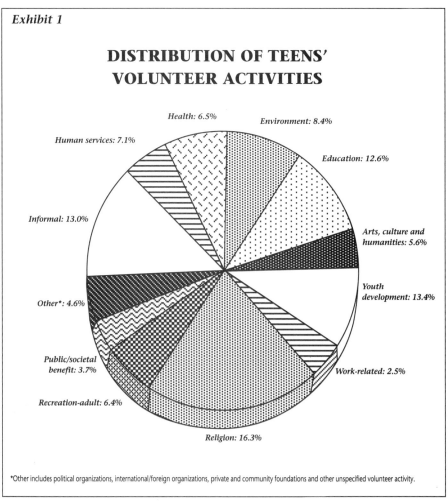

Exhibit 1

DISTRIBUTION OF TEENS' VOLUNTEER ACTIVITIES

Health: 6.5%

Environment: 8.4%

Human services: 7.1%

Education: 12.6%

Informal: 13.0%

Arts, culture and humanities: 5.6%

Other*: 4.6%

Youth development: 13.4%

Public/societal benefit: 3.7%

Work-related: 2.5%

Recreation-adult: 6.4%

Religion: 16.3%

*Other includes political organizations, international/foreign organizations, private and community foundations and other unspecified volunteer activity.

(Source: Volunteering and Giving Among American Teenagers: 1996. Independent Sector, Washington, D.C., 1997.)

- You get a chance to learn about various careers.
- You gain experience that can help in school and can lead to college admission and college scholarships as well as future careers.

VOLUNTEER FOR WHAT?

You can volunteer in a wide variety of activities. To get a picture of how teen volunteering is spread among various categories, see Exhibit 1.

WHO SAYS YOU HAVE TO "VOLUNTEER"?

Is "volunteering" for community service required in your school? It is if you live in the state of Maryland or in the city of Atlanta, Georgia. In fact, in many school districts across the United States you cannot receive your high school diploma unless you have spent a certain number of hours in community service. The number of hours varies.

Who makes the rule? In Maryland, the only state so far to require every high school student to perform community service, it is the Maryland State Department of Education. In most school districts, it is the board of education, which usually sets policies that meet the standards of the community.

If you have to do it, is it voluntary? And is it legal to make you do it? One family didn't think so. In 1994, the parents of Daniel Immediato, a 17-year-old senior at Rye Neck High School in Mamaroneck, New York, sued in federal court to keep Daniel's school from requiring him to spend 40 hours in community service before he could graduate.

Daniel's parents said the requirement interfered with their right to raise their child, that it violated Daniel's privacy rights, and that it was a violation of the Thirteenth Amendment to the U. S. Constitution. That amendment says:

> Neither slavery nor involuntary servitude, except as a punishment for
> a crime whereof the party shall have been duly convicted, shall exist
> within the United States, or any place subject to their jurisdiction.

The requirement for community service, said the Immediatos, imposed involuntary servitude on Daniel.

In its defense, the Rye Neck School Board argued that what it wanted was to get the students out into the community to see what goes on in the outside world. In the process, said the board, students would find out what it was like to have to dress appropriately for a job, be on time somewhere and have other people dependent on them. The emphasis was not on what the community would gain, it was on what the student would learn.

The court decided the school system was right. The Immediatos appealed. The U.S. Court of Appeals for the Second Circuit upheld the decision. The Immediatos asked the U.S. Supreme Court to hear the case. It turned down the request, as it does many appeals, without stating its reason for refusing.

CHAPTER ONE

What Types of Animals, and Who Deals with Them?

*T*he animal world is a big one. Nearly 1 million different species of animals live on Earth. The vast majority of them—more than 800,000 different kinds—are insects. Others are fish (about 30,000 species), birds (more than 9,000), reptiles (about 6,000), amphibians (about 3,000), and mammals (also about 3,000 species). The mammals include human beings.

For centuries, humans have tamed or domesticated such animals as horses, dogs, camels and elephants so they could help hunt or carry, or pull heavy loads. We also domesticate animals and keep them on farms so we can drink their milk, eat their eggs, weave their wool or use them for food.

Traditionally, humans have hunted animals in the wild for sport, food or clothing. We have trained animals as pets to keep us company at home and give us outlets for our love. We've captured animals and put them in zoos and aquariums so we could study and admire them.

The only animals we will have in the future will be the descendants of those we have today.

CONSERVATION AND PROTECTION

In more recent times, we have begun to realize that the only animals we will have in the future will be the descendants of those we have today. So we must conserve and protect them. We have put some limits on the number of

(V. Harlow)

Of the 3,000 different species of mammals in the world, people have learned to domesticate many. Originating in Tibet as a guard dog, the Lhasa Apso breed is popular throughout the United States and abroad.

animals we kill for sport. We have created wildlife preserves and national parks where animals can live undisturbed. We have built zoos and aquariums in which they can spend their captive lives in settings as much like their natural living conditions as possible.

The conservation and protection of animals is a field with a wide variety of career opportunities.

THREE KINDS OF CAREERS

There are many different kinds of people who work with animals on a daily basis. The one you are probably most familiar with is the *veterinarian*. He or she is educated to be an animal doctor—formally known as a Doctor of Veterinary Medicine or DVM, and informally known as "the vet." If you have pets of any kind, you probably have a vet who takes care of them whenever they need vaccinations or are sick or injured. Veterinarians are everywhere—in the city, town and country—because pets are everywhere. Treating pets is their biggest business. Most veterinarians run animal hospitals and boarding kennels as part of their services.

But vets whose medical practice is in small towns or rural areas care not only for pets but also for horses, cows, pigs, chickens and geese—virtually every kind of animal found on a farm. And while you usually take your pet to the vet, the farm animals have the vet come to them. Caring for and treating livestock is important work, because animal diseases can be dangerous not only to the animals but to human beings as well.

Another type of animal expert is the *zoologist.* To work in zoology, which is the science or study of animal life, an advanced degree such as a doctorate is not required. But many zoologists have earned master's degree or Ph.D's. In fact, this field of science is so broad that most zoologists specialize. *Entomologists* deal with insects; *ornithologists,* birds; *herpetologists,* reptiles and amphibians. Other zoologists concentrate on *genetics* (the science of heredity), *embryology* (the development of growth stages), and even *animal psychology* (the study of behavior). These are just a few among a dozen or more specialties that you may find interesting if you are thinking about caring for animals.

Fortunately, you don't have to be an expert to be an *animal lover,* and many experts rely on animal lovers to help them do their jobs. As a result, many animal lovers build up wide experience with animals by volunteering in the operation of city and town dog pounds and other animal shelters. They run programs that help find homes for unwanted pets, and they care for those animals nobody wants.

WHERE ANIMAL LOVERS WORK—AND WHERE YOU CAN, TOO

Where do all these people work? And where are there opportunities for you to volunteer? Think about three places.

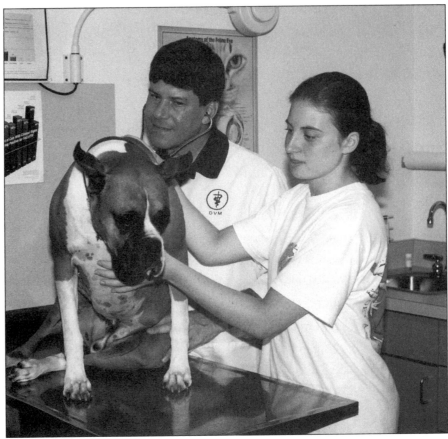

(V. Harlow)

If you enjoy working with animals, you may want to volunteer at a veterinary hospital. At the East Haddam Veterinary Clinic in Connecticut, Dr. Paul Urband is assisted by teenager Renée Ferrucci, as he performs a physical exam on Bart.

Animal Hospitals

Some veterinarians are glad to get teenagers who volunteer. If you are interested in caring for pets—for dogs, cats, gerbils, hamsters, parakeets and so on—your own vet may welcome your help. But remember, an animal hospital is a business. It is not a nonprofit organization in the usual sense. It is out to make a profit. So if you donate your time, rather than working for pay, you are helping it make its profit. In short, if you volunteer in a typical veterinarian's office or hospital, it is really more for your own good—for the experience you will gain—rather than for service to the community.

Zoos and Aquariums

These are usually nonprofit organizations, and most of them encourage volunteers of all ages. In fact, many could not keep their doors open if they had to pay for all the help it takes to run them. In a zoo or aquarium, your concern is in caring not for pets but for wild animals.

Animal Shelters and Pounds

These are the places where stray animals—usually dogs and cats—are kept while animal lovers try to find homes for them. Like zoos and aquariums, these are nonprofit. In fact, pounds are usually run by town or city governments. They, too, depend on volunteer help.

CHAPTER TWO

What You'll Do as a Volunteer

*I*f you want to volunteer in the animal world, you can start young. Volunteers as young as 11 or 12 are active as Kennel Kids in some dog pounds and in such programs as Tait's Every Animal Matters (TEAM), which spays and neuters stray cats and dogs and finds homes for unwanted pets. Some organizations, on the other hand, want you to be at least 15 or 16 before they let you start as a volunteer. It all depends on what you'll be doing.

If you volunteer in a zoo, aquarium, animal rescue shelter or dog pound, you will play a vital part in the operation. Why? Because all such operations have budget problems. Without volunteers, both teen and adult, they could never make ends meet. In effect, as a volunteer you are an extension of the paid staff. So the time you contribute saves them from having to hire someone to do what you do.

It's so satisfying trying to help a place like this. You see, here they don't put anything to sleep. Nothing—nothing goes to sleep. We have a dog up front that's been here for seven years.
—Colleen Adams,
Animal Shelter Teen Volunteer

And don't forget, although you are not being paid, the responsibility you are given is vital to the facility's operation. You make it fun as well as informative for visitors to go there. You help protect its animals. Your commitment to what you do helps keep the operation going.

(V. Harlow)

*If you volunteer at a horse farm or riding stable, part of your job will
be to groom the horses. Monique Corriveau began volunteering at this
riding stable in Westbrook, Connecticut, because she was interested in
learning more about animals.*

(Courtesy: Kristin Elliott/High Hopes)

When you volunteer to care for animals, you might not always work directly with them. At High Hopes Therapeutic Riding Center in Old Lyme, Connecticut, part of your day might include a "behind-the-scenes" job like moving hay into the horses' stables.

Consider four types of work that you can do as a volunteer caring for animals: jobs where you deal almost entirely with the animals themselves, jobs where you also interact with people, jobs in the organization's administration, and jobs on the technical side.

WORKING WITH THE ANIMALS

You might call these the behind-the-scenes jobs. Let's look at what you might do in some typical settings:

Horse Stables

You muck out stables. That is, you shovel out the manure. You groom, feed and water horses. You exercise them by walking them. You ride them if possible. You wrap leg injuries. Beyond working with the horses themselves, you clean up fields and clear out trails, and you paint barns and fences. You haul bales of hay and straw. As Patty Wahlers, president of Humane Organization Representing Suffering Equines (HORSE) of Connecticut, puts it, "You do whatever needs to be done."

In a rescue station, you will find that many horses come in afraid of people. Their psyches are bruised. You find out which ones hate stalls, because they have been "overstalled," and you work with them in the open running shed.

Many horses come in afraid of people. Their psyches are bruised.

"YOU CAN'T BELIEVE IT'S THE SAME HORSE"

"At HORSE," explains volunteer and high school junior Michelle Dahl, "we get horses that have been abused and neglected."

"It's really neat to see them start off," continues Dahl. "Often the vet predicts that they're going to die over the weekend because they're suffering from malnutrition. But we help them make a comeback and find a good home for them. It's really nice. We take before and after pictures. And looking back at the pictures, you can't believe it's the same horse anymore."

A veterinarian teaches you how to massage a horse's muscular problems and clean and treat skin sores. Most of all, you find that horses that are being rescued need plenty of tender loving care, with buckets of carrots and, as HORSE volunteer Michelle Dahl says, "hugs and kisses and petting and time."

You can help not only at veterinarians' offices and at rescue stations. Across the country, numbers of stables offer therapeutic riding for all ages. Therapeutic riding is a special program in which mentally, physically and emotionally handicapped children and adults are given the opportunity to learn horsemanship. The goal of such training is to improve self-confidence and physical strength and skills. Many such programs welcome volunteer help. "We start them quite young, under 14," says Pauline Knoll, volunteer coordinator at High Hopes Therapeutic Riding, Inc., in Old Lyme, Connecticut. "In our Youth Equestrian Apprenticeship, our YEA program, they work directly with the supervisor, learning all aspects of horse care, barn care, cleaning saddles, bridles, etc.—everything about what it means to have a horse and be responsible for the upkeep and the maintenance of the horse and its good health and so on.

"Then when they reach 14, they can work directly with the program. Many of the youngsters like to work in the arena. They like to feed the horses, they side-walk or help in the barn with the preparation of the horses for the lessons, with the grooming and tacking and mucking out the stalls and all of that. Many of them come in after school and do that kind of thing."

Knoll says some teenagers like to help with the office work, handling such things as computer input and mailings. "They also help us," she says, "with special events and decorating for parties that are going to be held here. Just recently, we had a hoedown. We had line dancing in the arena and we had a DJ here and the kids helped with the decorations for that. They created a big banner with each of the horses—we have 21—pictured on it in all colors. And that evening they helped with the food. And they danced. That was a social event."

Teen volunteers are especially welcome at a therapeutic riding stable's summer camp. "The teens come usually for a week at a time," says Pauline Knoll. "They work directly with the horses from 9:00 A.M. until about noon, doing all the grooming and tacking and riding and so on. So the volunteers are with the campers the whole time they are working with the horses, and then they help them with other activities in the afternoon. They have swimming and tennis or crafts or whatever else is going on. And many of them work one or two or three weeks at a time, assisting the campers. It's all equestrian-related, and it's all voluntary."

Aquarium

You check water chemistry—to be sure the pH balance is right and no outbursts of algae or bacteria are occurring. You scrub the tanks and change the water in them. You prepare food and feed the fish and invertebrates. You become a good pal of sea horses and skates as you clean them with a disinfectant called Betadine to help them recover from bites and other wounds. If the aquarium is a large one, you might "shadow" seals and other aquarium mammals. Shadowing means you follow them and make notes on their habits and behavior as they swim through their streams or channels or cruise their tanks. Your observations help with feeding and maintaining the health of the animals.

Zoo

A zoo volunteer, Jeremy Schimidt, described the four areas or "stations" at which he was trained to work. "One was the 'world of wildlife' building," he said. "We had all the educational tools there—microscopes and displays and places where you can read to children. We would take them on a tour of the building and answer questions and just throw in any information we had.

"The second station was the sales cart. When we worked there, we were selling various kinds of booklets—mostly on the field trips the zoo offers.

They bring out this huge cart and they set out the bio facts. Bio facts would be anything that used to be attached to a living being—a feather from a bird, or a hoof from a zebra, a skull from a chimpanzee, anything. They let the public actually step up and touch them and learn about them. Those kids really discuss the bio facts with the public.

—Tiffany Vanderwerf,
Volunteer coordinator, Buffalo Zoo

(Bernard Ryan, Jr.)

At the dog pound, high school freshman Colleen Adams volunteers at the Danbury (CT) Animal Welfare Society, exercising dogs on Saturday and Sunday afternoons.

"Then the third was the conservation cart, where we had materials on all kinds of environmental issues and we would discuss them and do demonstrations. For instance, we did a whole demonstration on the man-made materials and natural materials that will dissolve, so we were able to let them see how they could help save landfill space. And we used plastic wood to show them how much better that can be than using up our resources of standard lumber.

"The fourth station was the animal contact pens. This was animal handling. We'd use a bio fact chart that helped us describe the animals, and we had a lot of animal artifacts that we could show. And we'd handle the actual animals and discuss their habits and characteristics."

Jeremy adds, with a mischievous grin, "Last year in the animal contact pens, we were able to pretty much resist opening the gates."

Children's Zoo

You help by cleaning the cages of smaller animals, such as snakes, geckos, rabbits, ferrets, hedgehogs, turtles, tortoises and parrots. But don't expect to be invited to clean the cages of larger wild animals. That job is reserved for paid staff professionals.

Town Dog Pound

You clean out cages and brush and groom the dogs. You also train dogs in the basic commands: "Stay." "Sit." "Come."

You also learn to do some basic dog therapy, helping dogs that have been abused or abandoned to regain their confidence in people. How? "You start feeding them treats out of your hand," explains Colleen Adams, teen volunteer at a dog pound. "They come to you because they want the food. And then they feel more confident because they find out you're not going to smack them or something. I really like to watch them if a person has been bad to them. I like to watch them bounce back from their bad episodes and trust people again.

"We had two dogs that didn't trust anyone. They had been kept in a room, in solitary, from when they were born until they grew up. I helped them become so confident of being around people that they were able to be put in a foster home. I really like to watch them go to a home and have a good life.

"I introduced them to their foster parents," adds Colleen. "These were pugs—the Chinese dogs with eyes that stick out of their heads, and teeth that stick out. At first they were so scared. But I worked with them and they got more confident. I was really giving them therapy, playing with them and brushing them. Dogs can feel that you love them. They can tell. And they can tell if you don't like them and you're scared of them."

Animal Hospital

You may even get to help prepare dogs or cats for surgery. For example, after the animals have been sedated, you shave them where the veterinarian tells you the incision is to be made.

Humane Societies

Across America, some 6,000 humane societies welcome volunteers who are willing to help animals—mostly dogs and cats—make the change from being animals living in shelters to being beloved pets living with families. This means taking dogs for walks, playing with kittens, feeding puppies—all the activities that teach a pet what it's like to live with people.

Teen volunteers face two obstacles, however. First, you must be available during the society's normal hours, between 9:00 A.M. and 5:00 P.M., Monday through Friday. That means you are limited to the time you have between the end of the school day and 5:00 P.M.—or, of course, the summertime when school is out. Second, for most—but not all—of the work, volunteers must be 18 years old and must be vaccinated against rabies.

The exceptions? Younger teens, without rabies shots, help in a number of ways. One is the society's foster-care program. It places animals in temporary homes. If their parents or families agree, teens may take home kittens and puppies, nursing mothers and their litters, and animals that are undergoing lengthy treatment and recovery from accidents or surgery. When they are old enough or well enough, they return to the society.

What else can you do as a teen at the Humane Society? You can help with the maintenance crew, doing the general maintenance and landscaping, painting fences and buildings, putting up seasonal decorations at the shelter. And you can participate in the many special events held during the year. Examples? You handle registration and seating at educational seminars. You serve as a counselor at a children's day camp at the shelter during the summer months. You help handle the public—the signing in, the lines, the paperwork—when people come to rabies vaccination clinics. You get out mailings, answer phone calls and help with the endless paperwork that keeps the place ticking. (See also chapter six, "Where to Find Opportunities", and Appendix C.)

INTERACTING WITH PEOPLE

You can take your interest in working with animals into volunteer jobs where you meet the public.

Dog pounds are usually open to the public on Saturday and Sunday. As a volunteer, and with adult supervision, you take dogs out of their pens, walk with them, let visitors see how active they are and whether they have learned any simple commands.

PLACING ANIMALS—A SALES ABILITY

"Placing animals is a sales ability, the same way placing anything is," notes Ellen Farrar, director of the Danbury, Connecticut, Animal Lovers Society dog pound. "You can say exactly the same thing in different ways, and one way people will adopt it and the other way people won't," says Farrar.

"You can say, 'Oh, this dog jumps so much he'll knock you over,' or you can say, 'Look, this dog needs some training because he's still very young and jumpy,' " Farrar explains. Because the teens tend to describe the dogs the first way, Farrar tells them not to talk about the animals. She feels they are likely to be too enthusiastic in their descriptions. Instead, the teens deal with the public by taking out the animals,and walking with them.

In a zoo or aquarium, you are a guide or *docent*. You conduct tours. You present information and answer questions. You explain how the animals live and function, where they live, what they eat, how long they live, the depth of their tank and the water quality (if they are water creatures). You are a lecturer and a demonstrator. You speak to all ages—from preschool kids to the elderly.

One day, for example, you take a hedgehog out of its cage. You're very careful getting him into the carrying case, because if you frighten him the stiff hairs on his

(Karen Kraub/Sedgwick County Zoo and Botanical Garden, Wichita, KS)

Fourteen-year-old Sarah Weihy, a Zoo Crew volunteer, shows a frog to a group of young children at the Sedgwick County Zoo.

back will harden into sharp spikes. But you know how tame he is, and as you show him to the crowd gathered around you, you let his long nose explore your cupped hand to find a few insects to gobble up. And you describe how he can roll up into a ball of spikes when he is really frightened. Your audience is enthralled.

My favorites? Hedgehogs. They're really neat and they're easy to talk about. People find them interesting, more than they would, say, rabbits.
                    —April Davis, Zoo Teen Volunteer

If you can work pretty much full time for half the summer, you may become an "Edzoocation Aide."

If you are 13 or 14, your city's zoo may make you a Junior Zoo Aide. One of your jobs will be to put on puppet shows for very young visitors. Usually the script of the show is recorded on audiotape that is played while you demonstrate with finger puppets or larger puppets. The subjects? Nature and conservation. Individual animals and their lives and habits. And if you're a Junior Aide who is good at face painting, you may find yourself painting little kids to look like raccoons, foxes or cats.

If you are 15 to 17, forget the "Junior"—you may be a Zoo Aide. Now you can take on one of several responsibilities. If you can work pretty much full time for half the summer, you may become an Edzoocation Aide. That means for five or six weeks you show up every day and function as a counselor at the zoo's day camp.

As a Zoo Aide, not only in summer but also in other seasons, you are out on the grounds as a guide. You help people not just to see the animals but also to come close and hold or touch those that they are allowed to touch. You're giving the public its real hands-on experience.

LEARNING SO YOU CAN TEACH

Asked what types of work she did during her three years as a teen volunteer in the Buffalo Zoo, April Davis said, "It really depends on what time of the year you're talking about. In the spring, for instance, we work in the education department, where visitors come to really learn about the animals. We have to be there once a week, on Sundays. We're there pretty much the whole day, from 10 in the morning.

"First we have a two-hour teaching session—a workshop. They teach us all about what the animals eat. Then we go to the kitchen and get all the fruits and vegetables and we make up the diets for the day for the animals in the education department. Then after we have our own lunch, we take the animals that are in the education department and go out onto the grounds with them. And we talk about them with the public for the rest of the day."

Your schedule might rotate you from the zoo grounds into the Children's Zoo. There you help the little kids—some very shy, some maybe too eager—as they have their first hands-on experiences with ducks, geese, rabbits, goats and sheep.

In some zoos, Zoo Aides become skilled in telling children and adults about exotic pets. This is a relatively new field of zoo work, as many people have become fascinated by the idea of keeping exotic pets but don't know much about them. What is a typical exotic pet? One example is the gecko, a small lizard that lives on insects he finds at night and can climb a vertical surface as smooth as a plate-glass window. If you are a Zoo Aide explaining that trick, you have to be able to hold a gecko and show its feet so people can see that each of its 20 toes has an adhesive pad consisting of thousands of tiny hooks. If you and the gecko are on good terms, it might even let you hold a magnifying glass so your audience can see the hooks.

EVERY DAY IS DIFFERENT

"Did I ever get bitten?" says Jeremy Schimidt, Zoo Aide teen volunteer. "No. No one ever was."

Jeremy explains that working at the zoo is a lot of fun because you get to meet a lot of people. "It's not boring at all," he states. "You may hold an animal any num-

(Continued on page 27)

(Continued from page 26)

ber of times, but it's different every time. The moods of the animals change. And the attitudes of the attendants in the zoo change. Every day is different."

By his junior year in high school, Jeremy had spent two summers as a Zoo Aide. He plans to go into medicine. "The zoo helped me open up with the community," he says, "and that's not something that you're taught in school. You get good experience in talking with people. It's like being on stage. I want to go into psychiatry, and that's very valuable."

In some zoos, you lecture more formally, too. For example, you move around the zoo grounds with a cart loaded with pamphlets and posters about conservation and biological as well as zoological facts—including such artifacts as specimens, bones, eggs and entire small-animal skeletons. You let the crowd gather and you speak about conservation issues, demonstrating how certain plastics do or don't dissolve in water and will or won't reduce waste in landfills or how the use of human-made materials can help conserve lumber.

GOOD FOR THE ANIMALS...
AND GOOD FOR YOU, TOO

"Our program lets you get experience directly with animals in a zoo situation," reports Tiffany Vanderwerf, the volunteer coordinator at the Buffalo Zoo in New York.

(Continued on page 28)

(Continued from page 27)

"If you're thinking of a career involving animals," continues Vanderwerf, "this would be for you. Or if you're thinking of a career dealing with the public, or children, this would be a great start, because you're actually out there with the public, presenting animals and their biological facts. It gives you a lot of public speaking and animal experience."

What you do is good for the zoo. "It helps out the zoo," she points out. "You get the zoo's message out to people by showing them what zoos are all about. You entertain and educate people at the same time about animals and conservation."

ADMINISTRATIVE JOBS

Maybe you don't want to handle animals or feed or clean up after them. Maybe you don't want to stand at a guidepost and talk to the endless stream of curious visitors in a zoo or aquarium. But you like to visit these places where nature and humans get acquainted and you want to help them. You can volunteer to work in several areas:

- If you have typing or computer skills and an aptitude for other office work, you will be welcome. You can help with inputting names and addresses on the computer's mailing lists. Frequently, envelopes need to be stuffed, and someone must operate the postage meter or put stamps on envelopes by hand.
- Like to raise money? Every nonprofit organization needs you for its phone-a-thons.
- How about recruiting new people? You can exercise your sales ability by bringing in new members and, equally valuable, new volunteers to join the force.

(Courtesy: Sedgwick County Zoo, Wichita, KS)

When volunteering as a zoo aide, you may be asked to do a number of different jobs. At the Sedgwick County Zoo in Wichita, Kansas, Bob Lee supervises teen shadow Lindsay Anderson as she feeds the hippos.

- Then there are all the books and collections of artifacts to be cataloged, shelved, stored and filed. Your hands will be welcome helpers.
- What about graphics and carpentry skills? Can you help build exhibits? Zoos and aquariums must continually promote their basic features. Several times a year, they set up special exhibits and events. Some of these may call for special construction you can help with.
- And don't forget the information desk and phone—another way to let your communication skills contribute.

(Courtesy: Bill Chambers/Sedgwick County Zoo and Botanical Garden, Wichita, KS)

If you volunteer at a zoo, your job may involve wide-ranging duties. Zack Williams, 14, is painting a fence at the American Farms, which is part of the Sedgwick County Zoo.

TECHNICAL JOBS

In a zoo or aquarium, animal hospital or veterinarian's office, you may find that you can do some of the technical work that supports the whole operation.

How much you will be allowed to do depends on several things, including how those in charge interpret local and state laws, as well as their insurance policies, how much science—especially biology—you already know and even how much your help is needed. So you have to ask. Make it clear you're volunteering, and don't be shy about saying what you have to offer.

Animal hospitals and vets, for example, do permit dedicated teen volunteers to help with culture analyses and laboratory blood work. They will let you develop X-ray plates that the vets have exposed, but in most states they are not allowed to let anyone under 18 operate the X-ray machine.

MEETING A VOLUNTEER

For a "feel" for what it is like volunteering with sea creatures, say hello to Eric Brainsky, a high school junior who is a volunteer at The Maritime Aquarium in Norwalk, Connecticut, on the edge of Long Island Sound. Let's ask him some questions.

Q. Why do you volunteer? What's in it for you?

A. I love working with the animals. I'm interested in marine science, and I get to learn a lot about different organisms, ocean currents, oceanography and marine biology all at the same time. And I get to work with the public and give lectures, so it helps me learn how to speak in front of people.

Q. What's in it for the aquarium?

A. They get a volunteer who's willing to work long hours—sometimes tough hours—without a break when we're very busy. And they get someone who is interested in the field and loves their work. And, of course, they don't have to pay me.

Q. How long are the hours?

A. Sometimes I'll put in from 9:30 to 1:00 on one shift, sometimes from 1:00 to 5:00, and some days from 9:30 to 5:00, which is a long day.

Q. What do you do at the aquarium?

A. I work at various stations, giving lectures. I explain the animals to the people who come in—where they live, what they eat, how long they live, that kind of thing. At the touch tank, I tell about each individual animal and even hand them to people.

Q. What kinds of animals?

A. Crabs, oysters, clams, skates, sharks, echinoderms—that's basically the sea urchins and the sea stars—and we have some egg casings. Then we have the gastropods, which are the snails, whelks, conches—the various mollusks, which are the univalves. And we have the two-shelled organisms—clams, oysters, the ones that are segregated into bivalves. We have horseshoe crabs, which are very gentle animals, not actually crabs. They're more related to an arachnid than crabs, although they're in a family of their own. And the crabs themselves—we have rock crabs, green crabs, hermit crabs, that's probably the most popular area that the volunteers handle in the aquarium.

Q. Are your talks mostly for children?

A. No, we get all ages. Kids, families, adults, camp groups, elderly people—I've dealt with people who are handicapped, some in wheelchairs, where I've taken the animals out to them. Mentally retarded people come in. We're talking about a real cross section.

Q. Where do all the sea creatures come from?

A. All the animals at the Maritime Center are from in or around Long Island Sound, unlike other aquariums, which deal with animals from all around the world. We specialize in animals from Long Island Sound and the surrounding area. For example, the river otters we have now—that's one of our newer exhibits—aren't from lower Long Island Sound but up the Connecticut River a few miles. We have one big stingray, which is in the animal and shark tank. And among the fish we have striped bass, sea bass, trigger fish and some black fish—also known as tautogs.

Q. Any disadvantages in this kind of volunteering?

A. It'll eat into your social life a little bit. I do have a paying job, and sometimes the aquarium will call, saying, "We need you this weekend," and I have to say no because I'm working or I have a report to do or I just plain have plans, you know, to do things with my social life. I feel guilty when I have to turn them down. The volunteer commitment is four hours a month, which is basically nothing. I've been doing no more than eight hours a month for a few months, because I've just been so busy with everything else. So that's one of the down parts.

Q. Any other downers?

A. Some days it's just so busy and you get a lot of little kids and they're screaming and grabbing and you have to say "No, don't put your hands in the tank" 200 times in an hour. And you get the same questions asked,—"What's that and that and that?"—Maybe 50 times in an hour and you have to go through the same spiel that many times. So it does get a little irritating on some days. Other days it's better. You need a lot of patience.

Q. Altogether, then, how do you evaluate your own interest?

A. I love it. I've always loved it. Some days I get very, very tired and I have to go in and deal with the screaming children and I say, "I want to go home." But deep down I love the marine world, I love the animals, and I enjoy working with the public.

CHAPTER THREE

What It Takes to Work with Animals

*W*orking with animals will provide you with challenging and rewarding experiences. As a teen volunteer, there are several items that will be required of you. These include:

- strength and stamina,
- commitment and attitude,
- basic skills,
- basic training,
- patience and a knack with animals, and
- good grades.

STRENGTH AND STAMINA

Working with animals is physical activity. It is tiring. You have to be willing not only to get tired but also to get dirty.

If you work with horses, you will probably have to get up at dawn so you can muck out a stable and provide fresh water, among other chores, before you go to school. If she is your own horse, you don't mind. If they are other horses—castoffs or animals you're tending for a vet—you have to tell yourself not to mind. You're doing it simply because you care for the animals.

If you're a behind-the-scenes volunteer in a zoo or aquarium, you will probably have to report as early as 7:30 or 8:00 A.M. on a Saturday or Sunday, so you can get the cleanup and feeding chores done before the place opens to the public. Then you work through a long day.

Suppose you are a guide or docent in a zoo. Again, you may put in a full day, most of it on your feet and speaking with the public. By the time you go home, you are exhausted.

(Courtesy: Maritime Aquarium, Norwalk, CT)

Volunteering at an aquarium may mean arriving early in the morning to feed or clean up after the animals before the public arrives. At the Maritime Aquarium in Norwalk, Connecticut, aquarist Vicki Sawyer oversees teen volunteer Doug Stevens as he works with the harbor seals.

We learn how to go into the animals' cages, take them out and put them in the carriers. We take them to wherever we're going to show them. We take them out and we hold them. We teach people how to touch the animals and we talk about what they eat.

—April Davis, Zoo Teen Volunteer

Handling farm animals takes strength. You may have to hold a horse's hoof off the ground while you clean and dress a wound. The horse may or may not be cooperative. You may have to catch a squealing piglet that has a mind of its own, then hold it while it squirms and wriggles as the vet gives it an inoculation.

In a "touching zoo," you will get plenty of exercise. After several hours of handling small wild animals—putting them into carriers, lugging them to where a crowd gathers to pet them and hear about them, returning them to get others—your muscles may be aching by the time you plop into a relaxing warm bath back home.

When I come home, my parents say, "Oh, they must have worked you so hard." I rest and eat and eat because I'm just so tired and hungry. But I know I am helping the aquarium with the things they can't get around to. I'm busy the whole eight hours that I'm there. But it's always neat stuff, and I'm always learning more.
        —Jessica Melgey, Aquarium Teen Volunteer

COMMITMENT AND ATTITUDE

As in any volunteer work, you can be sure the professionals will expect dependability more than anything else. They don't want to waste their time training you if they cannot rely on you to be there when you say you'll be there and do what you say you'll do.

What makes you dependable is your own interest in the work. Do you have an interest in biology? In animal husbandry—the science and art of producing livestock, which includes breeding, feeding, managing, and marketing farm animals? In veterinary medicine? In pharmacy and pharmaceuticals? In any or all of the many areas of zoology?

If the answer to any of these questions is yes, you probably already have the degree of commitment you need.

The professionals, incidentally, like to see their teen volunteers learn. "They get the satisfaction of watching you learn about the animals," says animal shelter volunteer Colleen Adams. "They can't pay for people to come and work, that's why you volunteer. But they like having the teenagers learn stuff—like it's not a good thing to have dogs locked up in cages," she points out.

*I've had a fish tank since I was a small kid. I've studied sharks
for years. I'm planning to go into the pharmaceutical field,
and keep marine biology as a hobby.*
> —Eric Brainsky, Aquarium Teen Volunteer

Any nonprofit organization that accepts you as a volunteer is much more interested in your taking responsibility than in your having previous experience with
animals. They can teach you about the animals. "The most important thing,"
says Tiffany Vanderwerf, who coordinates the teen volunteers at the Buffalo Zoo,
"is that they're responsible, because they do have schedules to fulfill."

You must be willing to be there, on time and ready to work.

Aquarium volunteer Jessica Melgey sums it up: "They just want to know that
you're going to be dedicated and reliable. That you're not someone who's going
to just not show up whenever you don't feel like being here. And they don't
want you to slack off and take advantage of being there."

What that adds up to is *self-discipline.* You must be willing to be there, on time
and ready to work, with a positive and enthusiastic attitude toward the place, the
other workers and—perhaps most important—toward the animals. Some animal lovers will tell you that if you are not enthusiastic, the animals will know it
even before the people do. And the animals will let you know they know.

The most necessary attitude with animals is not being afraid of them.

BASIC SKILLS

The attitude you bring is more important than skills. You don't have to have
studied a lot of biology or zoology. The most necessary attitude with animals is
not being afraid of them. You must be willing to handle them, clean up after
them, feed them.

One particular skill that is welcome doesn't actually involve animals.
Teenager Jeremy Schimidt, a zoo volunteer, explains: "When I filled out my
application, they had more than 100 people trying for only 20 spots. They
asked me how many years of biology I had. I didn't have any at that time, but
I had lots of experience being in front of people, singing and acting on the

stage. They like to get people who have experience in talking—people who are very cheerful. That helps their image."

"No skills are needed," says veterinarian Priscilla L. Kerbin, "other than a willingness to get dirty and a willingness to see what sometimes are very happy situations and sometimes very sad, and some people just can't handle that. The most important thing is a desire to be there, more than anything."

BASIC TRAINING

If you are working in a zoo or aquarium, you will probably go to a training session once or twice a week for five weeks or so. If you are working behind the scenes, this will familiarize you with the place and teach you the behavior of the animals you'll be dealing with. And you will learn about their diets and eating habits and how to prepare their food.

A LOT OF MEMORIZING

"You have to come in for six weeks in a row," says Jessica Melgey, an aquarium teen volunteer. "That eliminates your forgetting what happened last week."

"I was overwhelmed at first," continues Jessica. "I had to memorize which tank is which and what not to feed this one and what to feed that one. I also had to remember what time to feed each one. That's a lot of memorization, and those first six weeks were pretty overwhelming. But that's the standard time for my position."

In the process, Jessica learned a lot about marine biology. "Every time I learn something new, I get so excited," says Jessica. "I know what this is now, and I know where this is found and what to do when this is wrong. The learning is the most important thing I've got out of it."

If you are working with the public, your training will teach you what to tell zoo or aquarium visitors about the animals. It will also brace you for the typical questions they may ask. "The training goes into all the scientific information you need to know," says aquarium volunteer Eric Brainsky. "For example, you learn the Latin names, how to handle the public and how to handle emergencies. If you've never known anything about it, you might have a harder time."

Emily Hudson, another aquarium volunteer, looks at it another way. "Anybody can really do it as long as you try hard," she says. "They give you the training sessions. You don't need to be great at science or anything. Just pay attention, and they help you through it."

We're looking for a little bit of animal experience. A lot of it can be experience with pets. If they don't have much experience and they're not afraid, then they get a lot of it here, because before they actually go out with the public they go through a training session.

**—Tiffany Vanderwerf,
Volunteer Coordinator, Buffalo Zoo**

Or suppose you're working in a vet's animal hospital and you are going to help prepare a dog for surgery. The vet will teach you how to clean and disinfect your hands thoroughly and how to clip fur and shave the dog's skin after the patient has been tranquilized. Because all animals carry countless microorganisms on their skins, you then scrub and wash the skin and cleanse it with antiseptics. You watch the surgery. You learn how to dress and bandage wounds. And you learn the laboratory side—blood work and culture analysis.

"Many people come in not knowing anything," says Michelle Dahl, teen volunteer at Humane Organization Representing Suffering Equines (HORSE). "We work with them and they learn about horse care. I'm one of the, I guess you'd say, mentors. I help the younger kids who come in. I do all of the vet stuff, wrapping the horses and such. Those who don't know how to do those things watch and learn."

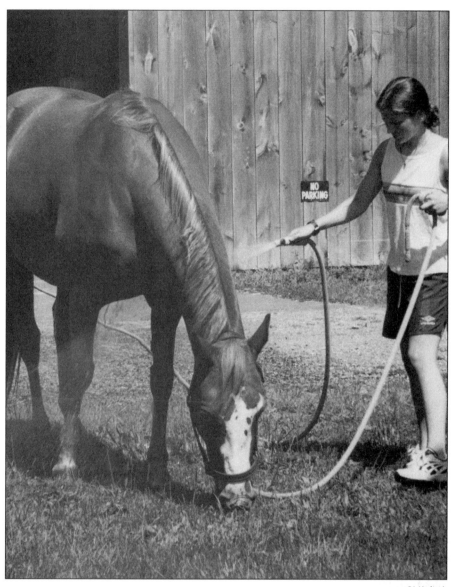

(V. Harlow)

Some volunteers must be trained before working with or caring for animals. At High Hopes Therapeutic Riding, Inc., in Old Lyme, Connecticut, teen volunteer Lindsay Welles was trained by other adult volunteers and staff members when she first began working there. One of her jobs is hosing down the horses after vigorous exercise.

"What qualifies the teens to be here?" says Michelle's supervisor, Patty Wahlers, president of HORSE of Connecticut. "We just want them to have a desire to work with horses. The basic training is that they have to work with me or one of the other volunteers. Once they feel comfortable, they can do things on their own. A lot of them have already worked around horses. Some already know a lot and they want to learn more. Some have never worked with horses. A lot of them have the desire to work with horses but they've never been able to. A lot can't afford to. And in most of the stables that you go to work at, they only want to let you shovel manure. And that's not worth doing. I want them to know something when they leave. And a lot of them will eventually some day own their own horses."

Wanting to know something is the key, says April Davis, a three-year teen volunteer at the Buffalo Zoo. "You have to want to know about the animals," she says, "about their backgrounds, their diets, their personalities. If you want to be a zoo veterinarian or a zoologist, you have to know all about all the animals so, when something's wrong, you know what it could be."

April enjoys using the knowledge she has gained at the zoo. She says, "I like it because I can go to a pet shop, for example, and look at the snakes or other animals and I know about them. I know what they eat. And other people go there and say, 'Oh, I want to buy a snake,' and they don't really know anything about it."

PATIENCE—AND A KNACK WITH ANIMALS

One thing you need is plenty of patience. If you are trying to train a dog or a horse, for instance, you must be willing to go over and over and over the commands and the routine until the animal gets it. If you are tired and frustrated, you can't let it show, because the animal will know it.

Caring for animals takes a certain knack. "Think of them as new friends," says Colleen Adams, teen volunteer in an animal shelter. "You never know how close you can get to an animal until you've worked with them hand on hand, or, I should say, hand on paw. Some are extremely loyal. You can confide in them and tell them anything and they can't tell anybody else. They understand you, but they're not going to tell anyone. And even if they could talk, they probably wouldn't feel like telling anybody. They're not like that."

GOOD GRADES IN SCHOOL

It takes one more thing to care for animals—good grades in school. As in most teen volunteer programs, you will be expected to maintain at least a C average. Drop below that and you risk being asked to leave the program by your school's guidance counselor or by the organization where you are volunteering .

WHAT IF YOU WORKED IN A ZOO?

Suppose you volunteered in the Sedgwick County Zoo in Wichita, Kansas. What might you be doing? What would you get out of it? How would the zoo, and its visitors, benefit by having you there? A chat with Karen Knaub, director of the zoo's volunteer services, gives you some answers.

"The 14-year-olds start in a program that we call Zoo Crew," says Knaub. "Here they work in small groups, behind the scenes in the zoo, doing cleanup-fix-up kinds of projects. Painting a fence, for example. That's a Zoo Crew project. They all do the same basic kinds of work, pretty much the work that the actual zookeepers do on a daily basis. The teens are kind of an extension of the zookeeper's right arm, so to speak. They go through a training program."

The Zoo Crew positions are filled on a first-come, first-served basis each summer. The zoo takes a maximum of 36. "Some zoos take many more," notes Knaub, "but we have found that is what we can handle. So we rate them only for age at that point—they must be at least 14 years old. And they must come to an orientation. We encourage them to bring a parent or guardian to the orientation."

Then, the following summer, those teens can apply for the Shadow Program. This is selective, says Knaub. To qualify, you have to go through an interview. "We set up tables with keepers who represent our American Farm area," she says, "or our North American Prairie area, or the African Veldt area, and they interview one teenager at a time with a list of questions that ask them about their experience, their goals, their schedules, that sort of thing. They rate their choices and the teens rate their choices for placement and we try to place them one on one. We go down the line, but the first choice is wherever we have a match that is one on one."

In the Shadow Program, says Knaub, you do such things as prepare diets for the animals, groom some of the animals, carry hay and alfalfa, sometimes help with exhibit repairs, fixing something that is broken in the exhibit area. "A teen might prepare enrichment for some of the animals," she says, "so that the animals don't have to face that daily grind day after day just like you and I do. We all need a little diversification in our lives some time. Enrichment might be a special snack, or it might be bringing some branches into an exhibit that are new and that a black bear or a grizzly bear might find intriguing to play with. It might be giving a ball to a grizzly bear so he can play in the water with it.

"And then there's always some animal observation that goes on, some procedures that the teenagers are involved in, if it happens to work out with their schedules. It really depends on the animals. Obviously, the contact they are going to have at the Veldt with an elephant or a rhinoceros is going to be considerably less than what somebody might experience at the North American Prairie with a river otter or a white-tailed deer."

The teen volunteers get some very special things to observe and participate in, from time to time, just because they happen to be in the right place at the right time. The very first day that Tyler Debarea was on his assignment as a shadow volunteer in the North American Prairie area, one of the bisons gave birth. "He was able to witness the birth," says Knaub, "and had some direct contact with the calf. But obviously he does not get out into the North American Prairie and go nose-to-nose with a bison.

"We've had some unusual circumstances with the kids," she adds. "We had one situation which, again, was a first-day experience for a teen shadow, and the animal that was born died during the birth. So it was a dose of reality for the teen, who came to the zoo kind of in wide-eyed innocence thinking that he was going to hold the warm fuzzy animals. He found out that there is another side to this."

The teens who become shadows, Knaub finds, often stick with it and continue as adult volunteers. "They are kids who have been interested in animals for a long time," she says. "At this point, they have some serious inclination toward a related career. So what you hear a lot is that they want to be veterinarians, or in some way to be animal behaviorists. Sometimes they don't know but they want to do something with animals. So what this experience gives them is a really unique opportunity to get close up and personal with that profession and see for themselves that it is not a glamorous life and that it is hard work. Rain or shine, seven days a week, those animals have to be fed, including holidays. They don't not eat because it is Christmas Day. Zoo people work in sleet and rain and snow and they are very dedicated kinds of people. And I think that offers terrific inspiration to kids at that age.

"We have also come to depend greatly on our teen volunteers for support during special events", says Knaub. "We have a full calendar, starting in March and winding up now with our Halloween event."

Halloween, she says, is "a real good example of how our teens support a special event. We use about 300 volunteers and I would say maybe half of them are teenagers from 13 to 18. They dress up in costumes, they act out characters, they drag wagons full of drinks around to other volunteers, they sell candy, they help us paint the props and set them up on the grounds, take them down when we're finished, clean up. Everything that needs to be done, they're there, chugging away, from the beginning.

"One of the things they love to do is help with our concessions. Every special event has the usual popcorn and candy, soft drinks, pretzels, all that stuff. The 14- or 15-year-old teenager who is too young to get a job is going to get wonderful experience operating the soft-drink stand or making the cones and having to make change and serve the public and learn good relations skills. We find that a lot of kids work to get experience that they can put down on job applications for the first time."

Knaub points out that the zoo's volunteer program provides a positive experience for the teen and for the zoo, meeting the needs of the zoo and the needs of the teen at the same time. "When we started working with teenagers," she recalls, "we had to go through some stumbling blocks to find out what ages. We made mistakes along the way with taking them too young. We arrived at 14. And now we get many, many calls from parents and teachers of third-graders and 9-year-olds who are looking for the same kind of experience. And we don't find that that's suitable for what we do here at the zoo.

"But what I think is important from our perspective, and what we keep reminding our staff," she adds, "is that they understand that this is not baby-sitting and not people getting in the way. They are helping to train future professionals, and these are future members. In many respects, the continuation of our own job security can depend on the kind of experience that these youngsters have.

"One real important thing to keep in mind," notes Knaub, "is that it is the student who is volunteering. And so it's the student, not the parent, who has to be motivated to do this. The parent might think it is a really nifty-keen idea for their kid to volunteer in a zoo, but it is the kid who is going to be scooping the poop and getting muddy. So if that is not what the student wants to do, it is the parent who needs to come out and volunteer."

CHAPTER FOUR
What's in It for You?

*L*ike other volunteer work, caring for animals is an interesting way to meet your community service requirements, if your school demands such service. It gives you the joy of helping animals and helping other people who help them. It offers many other benefits as well. It helps you toward your future career. And even if you do not go into work with animals later on, you gain practical knowledge you can use all your life.

You are bound to develop and improve your public speaking skills.

CAREER BENEFITS

Some teens already know they want to work with animals—as marine biologists, veterinarians, animal physical therapists or whatever. If one of those is your goal, you give yourself a head start as soon as you start volunteering.

I get a lot out of it. I get much enjoyment, but I also gain a bunch of knowledge. Ever since I was a little girl, I've wanted to be a marine biologist. Working at the aquarium prepares me to do that in the future. All the staff people I work with have helped me to learn about the field and really prepare me for the future.

—Jessica Melgey,
Aquarium Teen Volunteer

You gain another career benefit that is more widely applicable. If you are a Gallery Guide in an aquarium or a Zoo Aide explaining the animals to the public, you are bound to develop and improve your public speaking skills. That benefit will last your entire life, no matter what kind of work you go into. "There's quite a bit of public speaking," says Tiffany Vanderwerf, coordinator of teen volunteers at the Buffalo Zoo, "so it actually helps develop public speaking skills. It's an education tool for them to learn more about public speaking."

In looking ahead to a career, don't forget that any volunteer work with animals, like volunteering in community service, is well worth putting on your résumé. It looks good to any future employer.

SERIOUS ABOUT CAREERS

"We have had students who sincerely wanted to be veterinarians," says Dr. Priscilla L. Kerbin. "Most of those have gone on—three or four of them are vets, one is a pharmacist, one is in environmental biology—they've gone on to related fields. They were excellent. They really wanted to be here.

"They were wonderful and they went way beyond their requirements, stayed longer, both in hours per day and for years afterwards and were really interesting and fun to have around and wanted to be there and I think contributed a great deal to us. And I think we were able to contribute to them."

April Davis, a teen volunteer at the Buffalo Zoo for three years, says she got started there because she always liked animals—not just cats and dogs but the entire animal world. "I always thought they were really neat," she says, "so I always thought about becoming a zoologist. I just called up the zoo one day to see what they had going that I could do there and what I could learn. I got to do a lot of the programs at the zoo, so I know most of the people there, and they gave me a letter of recommendation for college that really helped me get accepted. I'm going to the University of Buffalo. There aren't any schools in this area that offer zoology as a major, and I don't want to go away to college, so I'm going to go into biology and take it from there."

LEARNING ABOUT CARING

When you volunteer to care for animals, you experience a special kind of connection with living things. Ellen Farrar, president of Danbury, Connecticut, Animal Lovers Society dog pound, thinks about it this way: "What's in it for the student is that they learn about caring. They learn about responsibility. They learn about a society that is not as caring as it should be with animals but that there are people who can care about the throwaway population. Caring is learned. It is taught. It's something that you learn because you are cared for or you care for something. Many of the students who work with us—not all, but many—haven't learned that. We give them a good responsible introduction to caring about living things."

Veterinarian Priscilla L. Kerbin looks at it in practical terms: "Most vets are in a position to teach any volunteer a lot of lab work and to let them observe surgery," she says. "They can learn to prep for surgery. And they can clean cages."

For a lot of teens, working here is a way to get a horse that they could never have for their own. They get to ride out on the trails. They can't do that the first day, but they can once we know this is something they're going to stick with. They earn the riding privileges.

**—Patty Wahlers,
president, HORSE of Connecticut**

At a dog pound or shelter, you can learn much about canine behavior. "You learn that some dogs are good and some dogs are bad," says Colleen Adams, a teen volunteer in an animal shelter. "You learn to be careful around the new dogs when they first come in. They don't trust anybody. Sometimes there's a dog that nobody but the warden can take out. Or maybe one that you've got to put right in his pen real fast after you take him for a walk, or he bites."

SOMETHING LONG-TERM

When you work with animals, you can find that there is something special in it for you. "A lot of teens," says Patty Wahlers, president of HORSE of Connecticut, "get something long term from taking care of horses, maybe because of what they've gone through—kids-wise, so to speak. Maybe they have had problems at home. Maybe they've even thought about—or tried—to run away. But they find out that horses definitely communicate very well with them. Horses can get through to kids better than I can."

A doctor who has practiced in teenage psychiatry for many years agrees on the value of a strong interest in animals: "Dogs," says Hewitt Fitts Ryan, M.D., of Tuscaloosa, Alabama, "make life possible."

OTHERS APPROVE

Also in it for you is the approval of others. Your teachers will be glad to hear about your volunteering with animals. They will think better of you for it. School-mates will be impressed and may want to join up, too. Your parents, brothers, and sisters are also sure to approve.

But most important of all is the approving boost you give yourself: You enhance your own self-esteem. You can't help but feel "up" when you know you are helping some other member of the animal family.

Every time I walk through that door that says AUTHORIZED *PERSONNEL ONLY, I feel like Wow!*

— Jessica Melgey,
Aquarium Teen Volunteer

Jessica's friends ask her why she gives up eight hours of a day—a whole day of her weekend every week—and doesn't get paid for it. "I tell them I feel like I should be paying the aquarium. At a young age, I'm getting a chance to do something I always wanted to do—something that makes a difference to the fish in the aquarium," Jessica says.

49

She admits she sometimes misses sleeping in on Sundays. "I have to be at the aquarium at eight o'clock in the morning," she says. "It's kind of a bummer because on a Saturday night I always have to tell my friends I have to leave a little early because I've got to be up at six-thirty to leave for the aquarium at seven-thirty. So sometimes I have to cut my adventures short on a Saturday night."

SENSE OF RESPONSIBILITY ... SELF-ESTEEM ... CONFIDENCE

Pauline Knoll, of High Hopes Therapeutic Riding Center in Old Lyme, Connecticut, finds that teen volunteers at the stable "gain a great sense of responsibility, for one thing. Knowing that the job they do is a vital one in terms of understanding what another creature needs, they get a greater appreciation of what's involved and just how much respect the animal deserves. They find out that the facility also needs their help in terms of taking care of the animals, being responsible for the way things are done, and that they are done in a way that everyone has to conform to in this barn.

"They also get a lot of self-esteem," adds Knoll, "because they develop relationships often with the riders, with other teens, with adults as well, because this is very much a team effort. When we have, say, a rider on a horse, they often need a leader. Very often they need one or two side-walkers. And then there are people in the barn who are support staff for all of that."

Third, says Knoll, there has to be a real understanding of the horse's behavior and what to be alert for. "So they really gain a lot of confidence in their own abilities," she explains. "For example, when the teens side-walk, they have to make sure that the rider is understanding the instructions for the lesson, that they are sitting correctly in the saddle, that they are doing the exercises or whatever is being asked of them, that they are safe in the way that everything is done, and that they indeed, again, respect the horses. Often, in fact, their knowledge of the horses assists them in working with the riders. And when the teens have that kind of confidence, they can offer the support and encouragement that the rider needs."

(Courtesy: Karen Kraub/Sedgwick County Zoo and Botanical Garden, Wichita, KS)

Working as a teenage volunteer at a zoo, aquarium or veterinarian's office on a regular basis shows responsibility and may help you start a career after you finish school. Tyler Debarea, 16, enjoys working with animals at the North American Prairie exhibit at the Sedgwick County Zoo.

HELPS COLLEGE AND JOB APPLICATIONS

Does caring for animals help you get into college? Jessica Melgey, who is very busy behind the scenes at a major aquarium, reports, "I haven't heard from the colleges yet, but it definitely gave me something to put on the application. It shows them that I'm there, at least three times a month, eight hours a day, giving my time when I have all kinds of other stuff going on, too. Hopefully it'll get me a job when I get my degree and they see I worked in an aquarium, I've got more experience than some other people might have."

HELPS START YOUR CAREER

Volunteering in a zoo, aquarium or veterinarian's office will help you learn so much that you might seem to be starting a career. It all depends on how much you want to learn. You can think of your service as an internship—a situation in which you gain practical experience under the supervision of a professional.

What kind of practical experience? Many of the kinds already mentioned, such as preparing animals for surgery, cleansing sea creatures with Betadine, or learning how to massage a horse's hip to relieve lameness—one of many skills you will need to develop if you want to become an animal physical therapist.

It does lead to careers. One girl who's been with me for nine years is now a 20-year-old in college and planning to be a vet. Another, who's 18, just started college and is in her first semester of horse management, getting her associate's degree. And one who's planning on going to college next year expects to become a therapist working with horses.

—Patty Wahlers, president,
HORSE of Connecticut

SHOULD YOU PAY A FEE?

In some zoos and aquariums, you may be asked to pay a fee for the privilege of being an Education Aide after you have spent one or two years as a volunteer Junior Aide.

If you're paying, you're no longer volunteering. If it takes you toward a career you want, however, it is probably worth doing, as it is likely to include equipment and manuals and even more intensive experience with animals. All of that, of course, will be good for college and job applications later on.

This teen volunteer works with sand tiger sharks and gives live demonstrations throughout the day allowing people to actually touch the marine animals.

(V. Harlow)

WHO WANTS TO KNOW ABOUT SHARKS?

Eric Brainsky enjoys speaking to large groups of visitors in a small city aquarium. "I'll sometimes wait for a bunch of people to come in," he says, "then I'll stand in front and scream out, 'Who wants to know about sharks?' And many kids shout, 'Me! Me! Me! Me!' And I sit them down and I explain about all the animals in the tank, which include sand tiger sharks—the larger sharks—and smaller dorsal and brown sandbar sharks."

The touch tank is another of Eric's favorites. "I hold the animals and hand them to people," he explains, "as I tell them about each one—the crabs, clams, oysters, all the mollusks. I'm interested in marine science, and I learn a lot about different organisms, ocean currents, oceanography and marine biology at the same time. I also get to work with the public and give lectures, so it helps me learn how to speak in front of people. I enjoy seeing the happiness on people's faces—you know, the kids who run into the touch tank and are willing to touch the animals. These are the marine animals that I handle every day, and it's the biggest deal in the world to let the kids touch these animals."

CHAPTER FIVE

Is It Right for You?

You've been considering some of the areas of caring for animals in which you might volunteer. You've thought about what you would be doing, and now you have an idea of what's in it for you.

The next question that comes up is: Is it *right* for you? To answer that one, you have to look at the good and bad sides—the advantages and satisfactions that you may get out of caring for animals, as well as the disadvantages and dissatisfactions you may experience. After reviewing these, take a self-quiz to determine if this area is right for you.

I really enjoy working at the aquarium. It's a different kind of science—a lot more fun than school. And I've met other teenagers who work there but who don't go to my school. It's fun because we all have the same interest, and we all like doing what we do.

**—Emily Hudson,
Aquarium Teen Volunteer**

ADVANTAGES AND SATISFACTIONS

Probably the most important advantage you will gain from working with animals is the chance it gives you to find out whether you want to concentrate on animals when you get to college and later in your lifework. If you're thinking about being a zoologist or a veterinarian, you can find out more about the field firsthand before you make a commitment in terms of your education. Finding out can save you time and money.

A huge advantage is that they do get experience in animal-related fields. If they're deciding whether they'd like to pursue that type of work, they will then know whether they want to. It teaches them responsibility and it teaches them how to deal with the public.

—**Tiffany Vanderwerf,**
Volunteer Coordinator, Buffalo Zoo

You can find out more about the field firsthand before you make a commitment in terms of your education.

You will find many other advantages in caring for animals.

- You gain the respect of people who understand what you are doing. This includes family, friends and teachers. Adults and peers alike respect the values you show in caring for animals.
- In most places—zoo, aquarium, vet's office or animal shelter—you can work flexible hours. The important thing is to know your schedule and give plenty of warning if you must vary from it.
- You make new friends. Teens who care for animals bond strongly. Someone you didn't know before in school, or from another neighborhood or town, may become a lifelong friend through your work together.
- You improve your self-image. You feel good about yourself and your accomplishments in learning how to deal with animals and the public.
- You learn how to handle responsibility. If tanks of sand tiger sharks, striped bass, stingrays, dorsal sharks and sea turtles are counting on you to keep their water clean and give them breakfast, you can't sleep in.
- You get a chance to move upward through more responsible leadership positions—from Junior Zoo Aide, for example, to Zoo Aide—and to help younger teens come into the system and learn it.

(Bernard Ryan, Jr.)

"What do I do?" asks ninth-grader Colleen Adams, who volunteers at the Danbury (CT) Animal Welfare Society. "I make animals feel more confident about being around people. You just start to pet them and they know you're not going to hurt them. They can feel that you love them. They can tell."

- When you apply for college and write up your experience in community service, you show how you have commited yourself to helping other beings, both human and animal.
- You see the difference you have made. "If I train the dogs, I like to watch them have a sense of, 'Oh, she said "Sit," we better sit down,' " says animal shelter volunteer Colleen Adams. "And I really like to see that the dogs don't come back. Just today I said to one kid who was taking a puppy, 'You better take good care of her. She got returned before and I don't want to see her back here again.'"

Colleen's supervisor, Ellen Farrar, sees another advantage. "The ones who work here," she says, "become very close to the other teen volunteers. A lot of the volunteers who have met here have continued to be friends. I know, because they tell me how this one's doing or where that one's working or how another one's been hospitalized. So they definitely gain new friends."

SATISFACTION: IT'S A GREAT FEELING

"There is the occasional screaming kid," says Eric Brainsky of his work at the aquarium, "but most of the people just want to learn. They want to pick up the animals.

"The satisfaction is wonderful, sometimes. Like when you just talk to the same kid about animals and he actually listens and you can see he's retaining the information that you give him. It's great—especially at my age—that I can actually be teaching kids and adults who come in.

"But you can't be shy if you're a volunteer," Eric adds. "You can't be afraid to reach out and tell people about things. That's your job. I don't recommend it if you're shy or afraid of speaking to large audiences or don't like dealing with people. And if you don't like people who don't listen, don't be a volunteer."

(Continued on page 58)

(Continued from page 59)

Eric notes, "You've got to figure that most people know nothing as they come into the center. Take the horseshoe crab, for instance. People think his tail is a stinger. They're so scared it's a stinger. Many times, an adult will comment, 'Oh, how can you let those people touch that crab with that stinger at the end?' And you explain how the crab's not dangerous. In fact, he's the most gentle organism in the tank. And you see the person reach out terrified to touch him and by the end of your talk they're touching the animal, they're holding the animal, they love the animal, they want to take it home with them."

Working around horses gives kids something to do with responsibility. It keeps a lot of them out of doing things they will be smart to stay out of—drugs and smoking and all that stuff.

—Patty Wahlers, president,
HORSE of Connecticut

DISADVANTAGES AND DISSATISFACTIONS
Now the bad news. There are some "downside" things you must think about.

No Pay
When you spend voluntary time in community service, you are paid nothing. You are giving up time you could be spending in a paying job.

Many teen volunteers have two jobs: the volunteer job and another that earns real money. One 15-year-old girl works at a horse farm on weekdays—early morn-

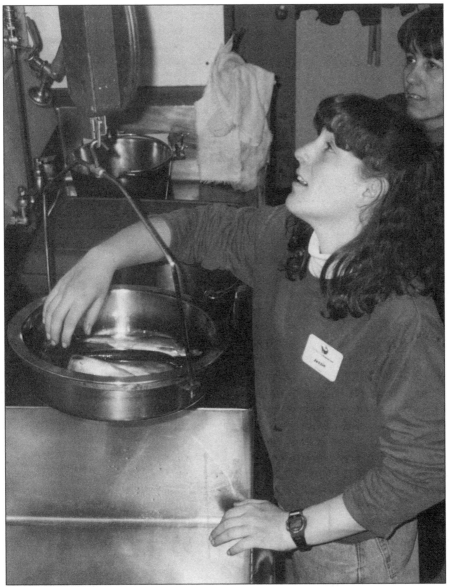

(Courtesy: Maritime Aquarium at Norwalk, CT)

Before volunteering for a job involving animals, be sure that the job is right for you. Working at an aquarium may find you behind the scenes, doing tasks like weighing fish to feed the harbor seals. Aquarist Vicki Sawyer trains teen volunteer Jessie Muhlin, stressing the importance of controlling food portions given at each feeding.

ings and afternoons after school—to earn the money for riding lessons there. And on Saturdays and Sundays, she volunteers at an animal shelter.

When you're volunteering two or three times a week during the summer and you have a part-time job, it's kind of hard. I had to figure out when I was going to be working at the zoo so I could tell my job that I couldn't work on those days. It was just a matter of working it all out ahead of time.

—Teen volunteer April Davis, Buffalo Zoo

Danger of Injury

When you work with any animal, you run the risk of getting hurt. It's a slight risk, but it is there. You can be sure that no one in a vet's animal hospital, zoo, aquarium or animal shelter wants to put you in danger.

There are times when you try to do something for a horse, like clean out a cut, and she kicks you. The horses don't understand that you're trying to help them. I've been bitten and kicked—beaten up a little by them. You learn very quickly where to stand to avoid those hooves.

**—Michelle Dahl,
HORSE Teen Volunteer**

Lack of Dedication

Some teen volunteers are dissatisfied when they find that not everyone in a training class at a zoo or aquarium has the same level of interest they have. "That was an annoyance factor," said one.

A veterinarian who took in volunteers from a high school vocational-agricultural program said, "A couple of them wanted to be there and were excellent. Others didn't want to be there, didn't give a darn and kind of spoiled everything for everybody. They sat on their chairs and never asked a question. You had to pull and push to get them to stand up. It became a hassle rather than a give-and-take situation."

Cuts into Social Life

Animal shelters are open to the public on Saturdays and Sundays. So are zoos and aquariums. That's when the largest numbers of the public come around, so it is when you are most needed. You have to be willing to give several hours of either day, probably at least twice or maybe three times a month. Furthermore, as you move up in the system, you will probably be asked to devote as much as five days a week for at least half of your summer vacation. If you're good at it, you find yourself in demand—your supervisor or the volunteer coordinator calls you when someone else calls in sick or the crowds are larger than expected.

Volunteering can help you get some of your social life into perspective. "I have a friend who yells at me a lot because I don't spend enough time with him," says one girl. "He says, 'You're never here.' Should I get him to come here, to my volunteer job? Oh, no. No way."

Physically Exhausting Work

"When it's really busy sometimes," says aquarium volunteer Eric Brainsky, "you're on your feet about 85 percent of the time. You don't get too many breaks."

Weather

Zoos and animal shelters are hot places in the summertime. If you're putting in six or seven hours on a Saturday or Sunday, you may be out in the heat all that time. The crowd can leave when it gets too hot. You can't.

"JUST COME!"

Veterinarian Priscilla L. Kerbin says the first requirement for volunteering in this field is a basic interest in animals. "I think most of the teenagers who have come to us independently," she says, "have come because they thought they wanted to be veterinarians or work in a related field. The best way to find out? Our answer has always been, 'Just come!' Spend a day a week. Find out whether this is really something you want to pursue or not. I think that would be the answer—if you think it's some place you would like to be, then you should spend some time, on a limited basis, to find out."

SELF-QUIZ

How do you know whether you're right for the job? You have to ask yourself a bunch of questions and see what kinds of answers you give. Here are some questions to think about:

- Do you have a broad interest in nature and animals?
- Are you squeamish about handling animals? Afraid of them?
- Are you willing to get dirty? Willing to clean up after animals?
- Can you discipline yourself not to handle animals or take them from cages unless you have adult approval?
- Are you at ease speaking to groups of people? Able to deal with batches of questions thrown at you by an eager audience?
- Are you willing to work long hours almost entirely on your feet and under pressure from a demanding public?
- Can you put in several continuous weeks of training, often more than once a week?
- Do you have the patience to respond to the same questions from the public, hour after hour, and keep your spiel fresh for each new audience?
- Are you ready to be treated like an adult—given the same responsibilities as adult volunteers?

- Are you willing to work hard to maintain good grades in school, so you can stay in the volunteer group?
- Can you give several hours each weekend to this activity?

If you answered "yes" to most of these questions, you are on the right track for caring for animals. Now think about what April Davis, a teen volunteer in a zoo, has to say. "You have to be outgoing, be able to talk to people a lot. You have to be a 'people' person, because what we do involves a lot of public contact. You have to know public speaking skills. I used to be real quiet and shy, but when I started doing this, it was a lot easier. It's easier to talk to people about something you like."

A MOTHER'S PERSPECTIVE

"When my daughter and I went to the aquarium for the first time, she was perhaps 14," recalls Emily Hudson's mother. "Until then, everywhere we had ever gone it was mom and daughter.

"But when we went to the aquarium, they gave her responsibilities. They treated her more like an adult than I did or would have. They gave her a task that first day, and it was like a window had opened.

"For a moment, I could see what she was going to be like as an adult woman. It was just one of those quick glimpses. I saw her behaving like an adult, being expected to be an adult. It was wonderful, because I certainly liked what I saw.

"You meet such great people when you volunteer. The kinds of people you meet when you are giving time and you're giving service and you're giving help tend to be wonderful people. We have just had such good times and done things that I never could have imagined before. It's opened up worlds. I mean, I never thought about petting a shark. I look at my children's educations and some of the most valuable lessons they've learned have been in their volunteer activities outside the classroom."

When Jessica Melgey, teen volunteer in an aquarium, was asked, "How do you know you're right for the job?" she had a ready answer. "I've always been the type of person who likes working with animals more than with people," she said. "Some other teenagers might volunteer at a hospital or a homeless shelter. While that interests me, and I have done work at soup kitchens and other stuff like that, I think I'd always come back to the aquarium because I have this deep-rooted thing for animals, and especially aquatic animals. That's basically why I chose the aquarium over any of those other places. And at the same time, it allows me to work with people, too, because sometimes when I'm out there feeding, people ask, 'What's this?' and it helps me learn more about myself and teach myself more than teaching them. Basically, it's the animals that drew me to the aquarium."

Jessica says she doesn't get any satisfaction from the public speaking side of aquarium volunteering. "There are opportunities for that," she says. "They call them interpreters. That's kind of a more intense training thing, and you have to really know everything about the animals that are there. I'm more of a behind-the-scenes type of person, and the only time that I'll really interact with the public is when I'm out doing feedings and they see me and come up to me and ask me questions like 'What are you feeding them?' or 'How often do they get fed?'—just little questions like that. And that's the extent of it."

Her greatest satisfaction, Jessica feels, lies in the way her volunteering has helped her plan her college education. "I'll major first in general biology, not marine biology," she says, "because I'm not sure whether I want to go into something in the veterinary field or if I want to stay with research. So I'm just going to go for a broad bachelor's degree in biology first of all."

But is there a point at which you know it's *not* right for you? "The hitch would probably come early, right in the training," says Tiffany Vanderwerf, who coordinates the teen volunteers at the Buffalo Zoo. "The training session at the beginning gives kids the first clue, when they're learning how to handle animals. If they find they're really just petrified, they may want to rethink their career choice or the direction they're heading in.

"Then, too," says Vanderwerf, "if they find they really don't like speaking to the public and they would rather just be in a room, alone or one on one, they may have to rethink the direction. Everyone starts out quite nervous about public speaking. If several weeks into the program they find out they absolutely dread speaking to the public, that's their other hint that maybe they wouldn't want to be doing this."

I know I'm doing a good job when the horse gets better or is healed, or when the horse starts to recognize me as a friend and greets me every time I come. That's how I judge myself.

**—Teen volunteer Michelle Dahl,
HORSE of Connecticut**

IMMEDIATE REWARDS

At the Danbury, Connecticut, Animal Lovers Society dog pound, where she uses teen volunteers, Director Ellen Farrar says, "The animals wait for you. You get immediate reinforcement, because these animals wait all week for the weekend.

"When a teenager they know comes, the animals dance for them. You know how you can really relate to an animal. A teen might choose an animal that's their special one, and just go off and sit with that animal for an hour. That's really what's very good.

"You take out one of these dogs and he just licks your face to death because he's been caged up all week. It's fulfilling. I mean, you're there, and you're rewarded immediately.

"We have wonderful happy endings. The kids are involved and are very excited about it, but the happy endings aren't happening to us. They're happening to the animals."

CHAPTER SIX

Where to Find Opportunities

*S*tart your search by checking with friends, relatives, parents of friends—any peers and adults who may know about opportunities to care for animals.

Then pick up your phone book and look in the yellow pages. Check such headings as *Animal Hospitals, Animal Shelters, Animal Welfare Societies, Aquariums, Humane Societies, Veterinarians* and *Zoos.* Check the yellow pages index. Scan it to see what else might be worth looking up.

In the white pages of your phone book, look for your state name with the words *Audubon Society* or *Humane Society* after it (e.g., *Massachusetts Audubon Society* or *Colorado Humane Society*). Call these agencies and ask about volunteer opportunities in your city or town or within reasonable driving distance.

Contact any of the following national organizations. Ask about opportunities for teen volunteers in their branches or affiliates near you.

American Horse Protection Association
>   1000 29th Street NW, Suite T-100
>   Washington, DC 20007
>   (202) 965-0500

American Society for the Prevention of Cruelty to Animals (ASPCA)
>   424 East 92 Street
>   New York, NY 10128-6804
>   (212) 876-7700

Animal Welfare Institute
>   Box 3650
>   Washington, DC 20007
>   (202) 337-2332

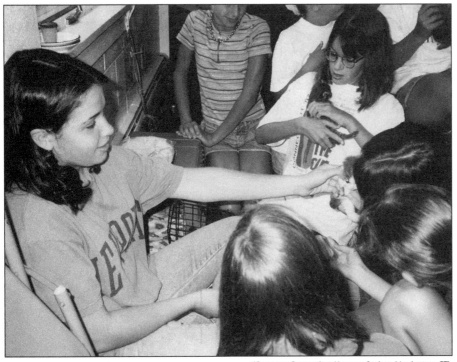

(Courtesy: Connecticut Humane Society, Newington, CT)

Teen volunteer Beth Kennedy volunteers at Connecticut Humane Society's Camp Kindness summer program. Beth teaches children how to handle and care for very young kittens. She also assists with vaccination clinics, pet facilities and therapy programs sponsored by the society.

Beauty Without Cruelty U.S.A.
175 West 12 Street

New York, NY 10011

(212) 989-8073

Defenders of Wildlife
1101 14th Street NW

Suite 1400

Washington, DC 20005

(202) 682-9400

Humane Society of the United States

2100 L Street

Washington, DC 20037

(202) 452-1100

The National Wildlife Federation

1412 16th Street NW

Washington, DC 20036

(202) 797-6800

The Wilderness Society

900 17th Street NW

Suite 300

Washington, DC 20006

(202) 833-2300

World Wildlife Fund

1250 24th Street NW

Washington, DC 20037

(202) 293-4800

Humane societies, for example, are found in more than 6,000 communities across the United States. Usually they operate shelters for homeless animals. Volunteers, including teens, help with kennel work, wildlife preservation, placing animals for adoption, and various other activities including lost-and-found animals and fund-raising. The national headquarters listed above and its regional offices (see Appendix C) can be helpful in directing you to volunteer opportunities. They work closely with the thousands of local shelters, many of which are run independently.

If you want to volunteer in a veterinarian's office but can't find one nearby, call information. When the operator asks, "What city?" ask for your state capital. Then ask for the phone number of the Veterinary Medical Association in your state. For example, the Ohio Veterinary Medical Association is in Columbus at (614) 486-7253. When you reach the association, ask if they can tell you of vets who welcome volunteers and who are located near you.

(Courtesy: Paul J. Fusco/CT DEP Wildlife Division)

Volunteers are always needed to help with wildlife preservation. Part of this young man's job for the State of Connecticut's Department of Environmental Protection's (DEP) Wildlife Division includes insulating a bluebird house for the winter season.

If you want to find out whether you can volunteer in your local dog pound, animal shelter or animal welfare society, give them a call. Look in the blue pages of your phone book, under the listings of city or town offices, and find the number for the *dog warden,* or for *canine control.* Ask for the person who coordinates the volunteers.

Chances are you won't get the volunteer coordinator the first time you call. Be sure to leave a message, with your name and phone number, saying you want to find out about volunteering. Ask if you need an application form and if the coordinator can mail you one. Or you may offer to stop by and pick up the form.

The person you want to reach is sure to be busy. So you may not get called back immediately. If no one calls within a few days, call again.

Any zoo, aquarium or animal shelter that is doing a top-notch job of serving the public is bound to have lots of volunteers knocking on the door. In fact, one teen volunteer in a popular aquarium says, "Sometimes the organizations are a little afraid of drawing too many people in. They're afraid that people might think feeding the seals is all fun and games. So they don't advertise it as much as they could and it's hard to get your foot in the door."

The answer to that, of course, is persistence. You must be determined. If you have decided on a particular place where you want to volunteer, keep at it. You may find that they accept applications only at certain times or seasons of the year. Make it a point to get your application in then. Ask if they have a waiting list, and say you want to be put on it. Write thank-you letters that follow up your calls. While you're thinking of them, you want *them* to think of *you.*

Any zoo, aquarium or animal shelter that is doing a top-notch job of serving the public is bound to have lots of volunteers knocking on the door.

I went to the aquarium just to take a tour through it. And I loved it. So I called the volunteer coordinator there, asking, What can I do? I ended up in one of their training sessions, and just started from there.

—Teen volunteer Emily Hudson,
The Maritime Aquarium,
Norwalk, Connecticut

SOME TYPICAL PLACES TO LOOK

You have to do some networking. If you want to work with horses, talk with people who ride horses and know horse farms. If you have a pet, ask your own veterinarian about his or her animal hospital and about other vets—as well as horse farms, animal shelters, the nearest zoos and aquariums. A friendly vet can probably give you lots of leads on places to look.

Here are some typical organizations (arranged alphabetically by state) around the United States in which teens volunteer to care for animals or to help others who care for them:

- **Therapeutic Riding of Tucson**, P.O. Box 30584, Tucson, AZ 85751; (520) 749-2360. This Arizona farm welcomes handicapped children and adults for horseback riding. Volunteers clean out stalls and help with the riders as well as with grounds work. Ages 14 and up.

- **Heifer Project International**, Route 2, Box 33, Perryville, AR 72126-9695; (501) 889-5124. From this Arkansas ranch, volunteers, including teens, send farm animals to poor families around the world. They maintain the ranch grounds and buildings as well as feed, groom and walk the animals.

- **The Humane Farming Association**, 1550 California Street, Suite 6, San Francisco, CA 94901; (415) 485-1495. Volunteers do clerical work, assemble information packets and distribute literature to help this San Francisco organization. Its goals include preventing cruelty to farm animals and protecting family farms from the competition of big-business "factory farms."

- **Sea Shepherd Conservation Society**, P.O. Box 628, Venice, CA 90294; (310) 394-3198. Office volunteers answer mail and provide information on the organization's work to protect marine mammals and habitats. Its goal is to prevent the killing of dolphins, seals and whales worldwide.

- **Morris Animal Foundation**, 45 Inverness Drive East, Englewood, CO 80112; (303) 790-2345, 1-800-530-8765. Volunteers help raise money for studies by veterinary schools researching health problems and dis-

(Courtesy: Kristin Elliott/High Hopes)

If you like to work with people and horses, consider volunteering at a therapeutic riding center. Here, at High Hopes, in Old Lyme, Connecticut, riders Joe Elnisky (front) and Pat Burns (rear) are guided by teen volunteers Jill Phillips (left) and Linda Almeida (right), as Kathy Fullerton, an adult volunteer, walks with them.

eases among zoo animals and pets. They also develop animal health seminars, sponsor such events as Ride for Research and Dog-a-Thon, and participate in county fairs.

- **FIDELCO Guide Dog Foundation**, P.O. Box 142, Bloomfield, CT 06002-0142; (860) 243-5200. German shepherd guide dogs are bred here. Volunteers raise the puppies, exercise and groom the dogs, help maintain the kennels and raise funds.

- **The Nature Conservancy.** This organization is determined to find and protect endangered species and their habitats. Volunteers work both in the office and in the field. If you are interested in volunteering, The Conservancy requests that you contact its local chapters, which can direct you to conservancies nearest you. For phone numbers of offices in every state, see Appendix B.

- **Sedgwick County Zoo and Botanical Garden**, 5555 Zoo Boulevard, Wichita, KS 67212; (316) 942-2213. Volunteers, ages 11 to 15, help zookeepers with their duties. Over 16, you are considered an adult volunteer and are given responsibility for the care and feeding of animals.

- **Audubon Zoo,** P.O. Box 4327, New Orleans, LA 70178; (504) 861-2537. The Edzoocator program, Children's Village, and Safari Cart use teen volunteers, 14 and up. The Zoo Corps starts at 16.

- **Atlantic Center for the Environment**, 55 South Main Street, Ipswich, MA 01938-2396; (508) 356-0038. Wildlife management in northern New England and Atlantic Canada is one area of this organization's effort. Starting at 16, you can intern in camps, research projects, canoe trips and workshops.

- **Heifer Project International**, Overlook Farm, 216 Wachusett Street, Rutland, MA 01543-2099; (508) 886-2221. Volunteers as young as 14 are tour guides and work with livestock and poultry in this operation that helps developing areas worldwide—including regions of the United States.

- **New England Assistance Dog Service**, Box 213, West Boylston, MA

01583; (508) 422-9064. Volunteers 15 and up work as kennel attendants and handle maintenance as well as clerical duties as guide dogs are trained to help the deaf.

- **North Country R.I.D.E.,** P.O. Box 312, Esko, MN 55733; (218) 879-7608. Teen volunteers lead horses and work with the disabled as they ride for therapy and rehabilitation in the Duluth and Cloquet areas.
- **Cape May County Park Zoo,** Route 9, Pine Lane, Cape May Courthouse, NJ 08210; (609) 465-5271. Junior zookeepers work with primates and cats and guide visitors through exhibits and educational programs.
- **Alley Pond Environmental Center,** 228-06 Northern Boulevard, Douglaston, NY 11363; (718) 229-4000. Featuring small animals, this Long Island nature center includes teen volunteers in its program of educational workshops and research in natural science.
- **Project P.A.W.,** P.O. Box 165 ESS, Binghamton, NY 13904; (607) 724-2241. Teen volunteers work as kennel assistants and do other animal-related chores for this program. The project's services include neutering, adopt-a-pet, and a thrift shop to raise funds.
- **Happy Canine Helpers,** 16277 Montgomery Road, Johnstown, OH 43031; (614) 965-2204. Cleaning kennels, feeding dogs and answering phones are among the duties of teen volunteers as this program trains dogs to help people who have physical disabilities. Experienced volunteers learn the training process and help with it.
- **Ye Old Therapeutic Riding,** 27560 East 77th Street, Broken Arrow, OK 74014; (918) 357-3622. Volunteering here includes grooming horses and leading them as physically and mentally handicapped children practice riding.
- **Washington Park Zoo,** 4001 Southwest Canyon Road, Portland, OR 97221-2799; (503) 226-1561. The children's zoo gives teenage volunteers an opportunity to work directly with the animals. The summer program is especially popular.
- **Concerned Citizens for Animals,** P.O. Box 1332, Simpsonville, SC 29681;

(864) 243-4222. Teen volunteers clean cages and take animals for walks at this shelter, where pet neutering is available.

- **Lichterman Nature Center,** 5299 Quince Road, Memphis, TN 38119; (901) 767-7322. Teen volunteers work as junior staff members in the wildlife rehabilitation center, helping injured wildlife return to their habitats.
- **Circle T Riding Center,** 9560 Hildebrandt Road, San Antonio, TX 78222; (210) 633-0678. Volunteers ages 14 and up handle tack, clip and groom horses as well as help with instruction of handicapped people getting riding therapy.
- **Discovery Museum**, 51 Park Street, Essex Junction, VT 05452; (802) 878-8687. At this wildlife center and children's museum, teen volunteers help with turtles, ferrets, rabbits and other small animals.

HOW TO APPLY

The application process in most cases is very simple. You may not even have to fill out a form. At a typical animal shelter, you just show up and say you want to volunteer. "We can always use a few more hands," says animal shelter volunteer Colleen Adams, "as long as you're not too scared of dogs and not too careless. In fact, you can't be too careful."

Don't worry—the adults who run dog pounds and shelters are quite cautious about beginners. They know which dog residents can be handled safely by new volunteers.

A zoo or aquarium is more formal. You will probably be asked to come in for an interview with the coordinator of volunteer services. Expect a few questions about your interests and whether you have been taking biology courses in school. Be ready to say something about why you want to work with animals. You might explain that you are planning to become a veterinarian, a horse trainer, a show-dog handler, a zoologist, an aquarist or whatever. Or maybe it's just that you love pets and want to take care of them—dogs, cats or exotic pets.

If you are interviewed, don't hesitate to ask questions. What kind of training program will you have to go through? How many meetings a week, for how many weeks? How many teen volunteers are in the program? How many of them are here at the same time on a given day or weekend? Is there a period of probation, and how long is it?

Let your interviewer know that you have thought about it. Make him or her aware that you want to know what you are getting into in the same sense that he or she wants to know about you.

Just try it out. If you're not sure whether you like it, or if it just doesn't work out, no one's feelings are going to be hurt. If it's not for you, you know it's not for you.

**—Michelle Dahl, teen volunteer,
HORSE of Connecticut**

GET A RÉSUMÉ READY

Looking for a volunteer job is similar to looking for a paying job: You want to make the best possible impression. Handing a résumé to your interviewer makes two points: (1) that you have been somewhere and done something, and (2) that you know how to think about where you have been and what you have done.

On your résumé, include your full name, address, age, grade in school and school activities (Key Club, drama club, sports teams, science club, 4-H Club, publications, etc.). And don't forget part-time jobs—from baby-sitting to delivering newspapers to mowing lawns and shoveling snow. You want the reader to see how well-rounded you are.

Asked for tips on where she advises teens to volunteer, the Buffalo Zoo's Tiffany Vanderwerf said, "To begin with, it's important just to have an interest in a given field. It doesn't have to be a zoo. The interest may be in a science museum. Any place like that is worth looking into. Almost all the not-for-

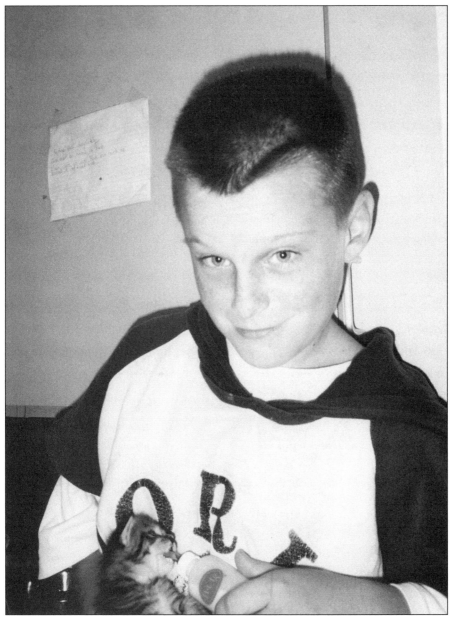

(Courtesy: Connecticut Humane Society, Newington, CT)

When caring for baby animals, you should have patience and you must be willing to clean up after them. This youngster helps to bottle-feed a newborn kitten during the Camp Kindness summer program at the Connecticut Humane Society in Newington.

77

profit-type institutions have some kind of volunteer program, and they usually need volunteers badly. Our own adult education program could not function without our volunteer docents. We really need them. And our teen volunteers are truly valuable, too—especially during the summer."

HOW DO YOU LOOK?

Remember the old adage: You get only one chance to make a good first impression. Dress for it, in clean, freshly pressed clothing. Make sure your hands and fingernails are clean. Shampoo. If you have short hair, it should be trimmed and well combed. If you have long hair, wear it in a braid or ponytail. Make it clear you know you shouldn't come to work with animals with your hair flying in the breeze.

Just find out what you'll be doing. You want to make sure you're interested in it before you commit yourself. Don't do something that you aren't interested in pursuing, because it's a waste of your time more than anything else. Volunteering can be a lot of fun if you find the right spot, so I'd definitely recommend it. It's been a lot of fun for me.

—Teen volunteer Emily Hudson,
The Maritime Aquarium,
Norwalk, Connecticut

GLOSSARY

Aquarist. A person responsible for maintaining an aquarium.

Blood work. The testing of blood to determine type, cell count and other factors that help diagnose an illness.

Culture analysis. The examination of living tissue grown in a nutrient substance to determine the presence, for example, of bacteria, yeast or viruses.

Docent. A person who conducts groups through a museum, art gallery or other exhibition place, usually offering spoken commentary.

Probation. A period of testing and trial for a person to determine fitness for a job or for school.

Side-walk. To walk alongside a horse on which the rider is a beginner or one who feels insecure.

Tack. Stable gear, especially the bridle and saddle used in horseback riding.

Veterinarian. A person who practices veterinary medicine, the science and art of preventing, curing and healing disease and injury in animals.

Zoology. Broadly, the science of dealing with animal life; more narrowly, the branch of biology concerned with animals.

BIBLIOGRAPHY

Adams, Patricia, and Jean Marzollo. *The Helping Hands Handbook: A Guidebook for Kids Who Want to Help People, Animals, and the World We Live In.* New York: Random House, 1992.

Boynton, Cynthia Wolfe. "Lifelong Romance with Horses, Caring for the Abused Ones." *The New York Times* (February 9, 1997), 2 CN.

Lewis, Barbara A. *The Kid's Guide to Service Projects: Over 500 Service Ideas for Young People Who Want to Make a Difference.* Minneapolis: Free Spirit, 1995.

Salzman, Marian, and Teresa Reisgies. *150 Ways Teens Can Make a Difference: A Handbook for Action.* Princeton, NJ: Peterson's Guides, 1991.

SUGGESTIONS FOR FURTHER READING

These three books are loaded with ideas on specific ways to serve your community:

Adams, Patricia, and Jean Marzollo. *The Helping Hands Handbook: A Guidebook for Kids Who Want to Help People, Animals, and the World We Live In.* New York: Random House, 1992.

Lewis, Barbara A. *The Kid's Guide to Service Projects: Over 500 Service Ideas for Young People Who Want to Make a Difference.* Minneapolis: Free Spirit, 1995.

Salzman, Marian, and Teresa Reisgies. *150 Ways Teens Can Make a Difference: A Handbook for Action.* Princeton, NJ: Peterson's Guides, 1991.

In the following group, the books marked with an asterisk (*) may be in the "Young Adult" or "Juvenile" section of your library. Don't be put off because they are "children's books." They offer good descriptions with plenty of detail.

Andrews, Roy Chapman. *Nature's Ways: How Nature Takes Care of Its Own.* New York: Crown, 1969.

Barber, Will. *Familiar Animals of America: An Illustrated Guide to the Wild Animals Around Us.* New York: Harper, 1956.

* Brooks, Bruce. *Nature by Design.* New York: Farrar, 1991.

* ———. *Predator!* New York: Farrar, 1991.

Budiansky, Stephen. *The Nature of Horses: Exploring Equine Evolution, Intelligence, and Behavior.* New York: Free Press, 1997.

Burton, Maurice. *Just Like an Animal.* New York: Scribner's, 1978.

Cooke, John. *The Restless Kingdom: An Exploration of Animal Movement.* New York: Facts On File, 1991.

* Curtis, Patricia. *Aquatic Animals in the Wild and in Captivity.* New York: Lodestar, 1992.

* Few, Roger. *Macmillan Animal Encyclopedia for Children.* New York: Macmillan, 1991.

* Fichter, George S. *Poisonous Animals.* New York: Watts, 1991.

* Gerstenfeld, Sheldon L. *The Aquarium Take-along Book.* New York: Viking, 1994.

* ———. *Zoo Clues: Making the Most of Your Visit to the Zoo.* New York: Viking, 1991.

* Graff, Nancy P. *The Strength of the Hills: A Portrait of a Family Farm.* Boston: Little, Brown, 1989.

Gray, Gary G. *Wildlife and People.* Champaign: University of Illinois Press, 1993.

Grzimek, Bernhard. *Grzimek's Encyclopedia of Animals.* 5 vols. New York: McGraw-Hill, 1990.

Makeham, John P., and L.R. Malcolm. *The Farming Game Now.* New York: Cambridge, 1993.

* McGrath, Susan. *The Amazing Things Animals Do.* Washington: National Geographic Society, 1992.

Moore, Peter D., ed. *The Encyclopedia of Animal Ecology.* New York: Facts On File, 1987.

Nowak, Ronald M. *Walker's Mammals of the World.* 2 vols. Baltimore: Johns Hopkins, 1991.

Parker, Steve. *How Do We Know Animals Can Think?* Austin, TX: Raintree Steck-Vaughn, 1995.

Pfeffer, Pierre, ed. *Predators and Predation: The Struggle for Life in the Animal World.* New York: Facts On File, 1989.

* Staple, Michelle, and Linda Gamlin. *The Random House Book of 1001 Questions and Answers About Animals.* New York: Random House, 1990.

In the reference section of your school or public library, be sure to find the *Encyclopedia Americana* or *World Book Encyclopedia.* Read the entries on Animals, Birds, Farms and Farming, Veterinarians, Wildlife, Zoos, and Zoology. Also check the "related articles" listed at the end of each.

The following books will help give you a broad understanding of volunteerism and opportunities in community service.

Berkowitz, Bill. *Local Heroes: The Rebirth of Heroism in America.* Lexington, MA: Lexington Books (D.C. Heath), 1987.

Buckley, William F., Jr. *Gratitude: Reflections on What We Owe to Our Country.* New York: Random House, 1990.

Coles, Robert. *The Call of Service: A Witness to Idealism.* Boston: Houghton Mifflin, 1993.

Daloz, Laurent A., et al. *Common Fire: Lives of Commitment in a Complex World.* Boston: Beacon Press, 1996.

Griggs, John, ed. *Simple Acts of Kindness: Volunteering in the Age of AIDS.* New York: United Hospital Fund of New York, 1989.

Luks, Allan, with Peggy Payne. *The Healing Power of Doing Good: The Health and Spiritual Benefits of Helping Others.* New York: Fawcett Columbine, 1991.

Olasky, Marvin. *Renewing American Compassion.* New York: The Free Press (Simon & Schuster), 1996.

Tarshis, Lauren. *Taking Off: Extraordinary Ways to Spend Your First Year Out of College.* New York: Fireside (Simon & Schuster), 1989.

Wuthnow, Robert. *Acts of Compassion: Caring for Others and Helping Ourselves.* Princeton, NJ: Princeton University Press, 1991.

APPENDIX A

Sample Volunteer Brochure

A typical brochure on volunteering, which you might pick up when you visit an aquarium, is this one titled "Volunteer Opportunities" from The Maritime Aquarium at Norwalk, Connecticut:

The Role of Maritime Aquarium Volunteers

Maritime Aquarium volunteers provide an expansive and invaluable service to the Aquarium. The group of talented and dedicated individuals functions in a critical role as an extension of the paid staff.

Volunteers' assignments are varied and range from administrative and other behind-the-scenes responsibilities to frontline jobs throughout the Aquarium and other areas visited by the public.

While the position is unpaid, the responsibilities entrusted to volunteers are vital to the operation of the facility. The Aquarium relies on volunteers to interpret and protect its marine and maritime collections while enhancing visitors' experiences. The volunteer's commitment is critical and greatly appreciated. In return, joining the volunteer program promises to be rewarding, challenging, and enjoyable.

Volunteer Opportunities

Volunteering at The Maritime Aquarium offers a level of involvement beyond that of the casual visitor. The Aquarium has volunteer programs for everyone—young and old, night people and day people. Those who work during the week can participate in evening and weekend programs or in behind-the-scenes activities.

As a volunteer, you become a member of The Maritime Aquarium family and learn more about the maritime history of Long Island Sound and its unique and wonderful marine life. Volunteer activities enable you to participate in and support the Aquarium's education and research programs while meeting and sharing time with people with similar interests.

Gallery Guides

Gallery Guides are needed 363 days a year to help visitors appreciate and learn more about Long Island Sound's rich maritime history and marine life.

They are the Aquarium's primary interface with our visitors. They staff the Seal Pool, the Open Ocean Gallery, the Touch Tank, plus other exhibits throughout The Maritime Aquarium.

Assistants

The special skills of Assistants are used to enhance the mission of The Maritime Aquarium. Assistants' roles include: staffing the information desk, helping with special events, preparing fish food, cleaning tanks, cataloging books and artifacts, assisting with office work, building exhibits and disseminating membership and program information.

Requirements: Training

All volunteers are expected to successfully complete the Aquarium's Volunteer Training Program. Attendance and participation in this course are vital to the integrity and success of the Aquarium's Volunteer program. There are eight classes scheduled Tuesdays and Thursdays over a four-week period. This classroom activity is followed by an 8- to 12-hour probationary period involving on-station training during which an individual rotates between the four key Gallery Guide stations. A uniform polo shirt and name badge, which are issued to graduates, are to be worn on duty. Upon completion of six months of active service, a complimentary membership is awarded.

Age

The minimum age for all prospective volunteers is 15.

Cost

A $25 registration fee is required for the Volunteer Training Program. This fee defrays the costs of training materials, name badge, and uniform polo shirt.

Time Commitment

A specific time commitment is expected from every volunteer. The commitment is established with each volunteer upon completion of the Volunteer Training Course.

APPENDIX B

The Nature Conservancy State and Regional Field Offices

Eastern Region	(617) 542-1908	Nevada	(702) 737-8744
Midwest Region	(612) 331-0700	New Hampshire	(603) 224-5853
Southwest Region	(919) 967-5493	New Jersey	(908) 879-7262
Western Region	(303) 444-1060	New Mexico	(505) 988-3867
Latin America	(703) 841-5300	New York Region	(518) 463-6133
Pacific Region	(808) 537-4508	New York City	(212) 997-1880
Alabama	(205) 251-1155	Adirondack NY	(518) 576-2082
Alaska	(907) 276-3133	Central &	
Arizona	(520) 622-3861	Western NY	(716) 546-8030
Arkansas	(501) 663-6699	Eastern NY	(518) 272-0195
California	(415) 777-0487	Long Island NY	(516) 367-3225
Colorado	(303) 444-2950	Lower Hudson NY	(914) 244-3271
Connecticut	(860) 344-0716	South Fork/	
Delaware	(302) 369-4144	Shelter I. NY	(516) 329-7689
Florida	(407) 682-3664	North Carolina	(919) 403-8558
Georgia	(404) 873-6946	North Dakota	(701) 222-8464
Hawaii	(808) 537-4508	Ohio	(614) 717-2770
Idaho	(208) 726-3007	Oklahoma	(918) 585-1117
Illinois	(312) 346-8166	Oregon	(503) 230-1221
Indiana	(317) 923-7547	Pennsylvania	(610) 834-1323
Iowa	(515) 244-5044	Rhode Island	(401) 331-7110
Kansas	(913) 233-4400	South Carolina	(803) 254-9049
Kentucky	(606) 259-9655	South Dakota	(605) 331-0619
Louisiana	(504) 338-1040	Tennessee	(615) 255-0303
Maine	(207) 729-5181	Texas	(210) 224-8774
Maryland	(301) 656-8673	Utah	(801) 531-0999
Massachusetts	(617) 423-2545	Vermont	(802) 229-4425
Michigan	(517) 332-1741	Virginia	(804) 295-6106
Minnesota	(612) 331-0750	Washington	(206) 343-4344
Mississippi	(601) 355-5357	West Virginia	(304) 345-4350
Missouri	(314) 968-1105	Wisconsin	(608) 251-8140
Montana	(406) 443-0303	Wyoming	(307) 332-2971
Nebraska	(402) 342-0282		

APPENDIX C

The Humane Society of the United States Regional Offices

Serving Maryland and Virginia:

> The Humane Society of the United States (national office)
> 2100 L Street, NW
> Washington DC 20037
> (202) 452-1100

Serving Illinois, Kentucky, Minnesota, North Carolina, Tennessee and Wisconsin:

> Central States Regional Office
> 800 West Fifth Avenue - Suite 110
> Naperville, Illinois 60560
> (630) 357-7015
> (630) 357-5725 FAX

Serving Indiana, Michigan, Ohio and West Virginia:

> Great Lakes Regional Office
> 745 Haskins Street
> Bowling Green, Ohio 43402-1696
> (419) 352-5141
> (419) 354-5351 FAX

Serving Delaware, New Jersey, New York and Pennsylvania:

> Mid-Atlantic Regional Office
> Bartley Square
> 270 Route 206
> Flanders, New Jersey 07836
> (201) 927-5611
> (201) 927-5617 FAX

Serving Iowa, Kansas, Missouri and Nebraska:

> Midwest Regional Office
> Argyle Building
> 306 East 12th Street - Suite 625
> Kansas City, Missouri 64106
> (816) 474-0888
> (816) 474-0898 FAX

Serving Connecticut, Maine, Massachusetts, New Hampshire, Rhode Island
and Vermont:
New England Regional Office
Route 117
P.O. Box 619 (mailing address)
Jacksonville, Vermont 05342-0619
(802) 368-2790
(802) 368-2756 FAX

Serving Idaho, Montana, North Dakota, South Dakota and Wyoming:
Northern Rockies Regional Office
490 North 31st Street - Suite 215
Billings, Montana 59101
(406) 255-7161
(406) 255-7162 FAX

Serving Alabama, Florida, Georgia, Mississippi and South Carolina:
Southeast Regional Office
1624 Metropolitan Circle - Suite B
Tallahassee, Florida 32308
(904) 386-3435
(904) 386-4534 FAX

Serving Arizona, Arkansas, Colorado, Louisiana, New Mexico, Oklahoma,
Texas and Utah:
Southwest Regional Office
3001 LBJ Freeway - Suite 224
Dallas, Texas 75234
(972) 488-2964
(972) 488-2965 FAX

Serving California, Nevada, Oregon and Washington:
West Coast Regional Office
5301 Madison Avenue - Suite 202
P.O. Box 417220 (mailing address)
Sacramento, California 95841-7220
(916) 344-1710
(916) 344-1808 FAX